SSAT LOWER LEVEL Mathematics Pr

www.EffortlessMath.com

… So Much More Online!

✓ FREE Math lessons

✓ More Math learning books!

✓ Mathematics Worksheets

✓ Online Math Tutors

Need a PDF version of this book?

Visit www.EffortlessMath.com

SSAT Lower Level Mathematics Prep 2019

A Comprehensive Review and Ultimate Guide to the SSAT Lower Level Math Test

By

Reza Nazari & Ava Ross

Copyright © 2018

Reza Nazari & Ava Ross

All rights reserved. No part of this publication may be reproduced, stored in a retrieval system, or transmitted in any form or by any means, electronic, mechanical, photocopying, recording, scanning, or otherwise, except as permitted under Section 107 or 108 of the 1976 United States Copyright Ac, without permission of the author.

All inquiries should be addressed to:

info@EffortlessMath.com

www.EffortlessMath.com

ISBN: 9781729217818

Published by: Effortless Math Education

www.EffortlessMath.com

Description

SSAT Lower Level Mathematics Prep 2019 provides students with the confidence and math skills they need to succeed on the SSAT Lower Level Math, building a solid foundation of basic Math topics with abundant exercises for each topic. It is designed to address the needs of SSAT Lower Level test takers who must have a working knowledge of basic Math.

This comprehensive book with over 2,500 sample questions and 2 complete SSAT Lower Level tests is all you need to fully prepare for the SSAT Lower Level Math. It will help you learn everything you need to ace the math section of the SSAT Lower Level.

There are more than 2,500 Math problems with answers in this book.
Effortless Math unique study program provides you with an in-depth focus on the math portion of the exam, helping you master the math skills that students find the most troublesome.
This book contains most common sample questions that are most likely to appear in the mathematics section of the SSAT Lower Level.

Inside the pages of this comprehensive SSAT Lower Level Math book, students can learn basic math operations in a structured manner with a complete study program to help them understand essential math skills. It also has many exciting features, including:

- Dynamic design and easy-to-follow activities
- A fun, interactive and concrete learning process
- Targeted, skill-building practices
- Fun exercises that build confidence
- Math topics are grouped by category, so you can focus on the topics you struggle on
- All solutions for the exercises are included, so you will always find the answers
- 2 Complete SSAT Lower Level Math Practice Tests that reflect the format and question types on SSAT Lower Level

SSAT Lower Level Mathematics Prep 2019 is an incredibly useful tool for those who want to review all topics being covered on the SSAT Lower Level test. It efficiently and effectively reinforces learning outcomes through engaging questions and repeated practice, helping you to quickly master basic Math skills.

About the Author

Reza Nazari is the author of more than 100 Math learning books including:
– **Math and Critical Thinking Challenges:** For the Middle and High School Student
– **ACT Math in 30 Days.**
– **ASVAB Math Workbook 2018 – 2019**
– **Effortless Math Education Workbooks**
– and many more Mathematics books …

Reza is also an experienced Math instructor and a test–prep expert who has been tutoring students since 2008. Reza is the founder of Effortless Math Education, a tutoring company that has helped many students raise their standardized test scores—and attend the colleges of their dreams. Reza provides an individualized custom learning plan and the personalized attention that makes a difference in how students view math.

You can contact Reza via email at:
reza@EffortlessMath.com

Find Reza's professional profile at:
goo.gl/zoC9rJ

Contents

Description 2

Chapter 1: Place Vales and Number Sense 9
    Place Values 10
    Comparing and Ordering Numbers 11
    Write Numbers in Words 12
    Rounding Numbers 13
    Odd or Even 14
    Answers of Worksheets – Chapter 1 15

Chapter 2: Adding and Subtracting 18
    Adding Two–Digit Numbers 19
    Subtracting Two–Digit Numbers 20
    Adding Three–Digit Numbers 21
    Adding Hundreds 22
    Adding 4–Digit Numbers 23
    Subtracting 4–Digit Numbers 24
    Answers of Worksheets – Chapter 2 25

Chapter 3: Multiplication and Division 26
    Multiplication 27
    Division 28
    Long Division by One Digit 29
    Division with Remainders 30
    Answers of Worksheets – Chapter 3 31

Chapter 4: Mixed operations 32
    Rounding and Estimating 33
    Estimate Sums 34
    Estimate Differences 35
    Estimate Products 36
    Missing Numbers 37
    Answers of Worksheets – Chapter 4 38

Chapter 5: Algebra 40

- Evaluating Variable 41
- Evaluating Two Variables 42
- Solve Equations 43
- Answers of Worksheets – Chapter 5 44

Chapter 6: Data and Graphs 45
- Graph Points on a Coordinate Plane 46
- Bar Graph 47
- Tally and Pictographs 48
- Line Graphs 49
- Stem–And–Leaf Plot 50
- Scatter Plots 51
- Answers of Worksheets – Chapter 6 53

Chapter 7: Patterns and Sequences 57
- Repeating Pattern 58
- Growing Patterns 59
- Patterns: Numbers 60
- Patterns 61
- Answers of Worksheets – Chapter 7 63

Chapter 8: Money 65
- Add Money Amounts 66
- Subtract Money Amounts 67
- Money: Word Problems 68
- Answers of Worksheets – Chapter 8 69

Chapter 9: Measurement 70
- Metric System 71
- Length 72
- Temperature 73
- Liters & Milliliters 74
- Kilograms & Grams 75
- Answers of Worksheets – Chapter 9 76

Chapter 10: Time 78
- Read Clocks 79

Telling Time 80

Digital Clock 81

Measurement – Time 82

Answers of Worksheets – Chapter 10 83

Chapter 11: Geometric 84

Identifying Angles: Acute, Right, Obtuse, and Straight Angles 85

Polygon Names 86

Classify Triangles 87

Parallel Sides in Quadrilaterals 88

Identify Rectangles 89

Perimeter: Find the Missing Side Lengths 90

Perimeter and Area of Squares 91

Perimeter and Area of rectangles 92

Find the Area or Missing Side Length of a Rectangle 93

Area and Perimeter: Word Problems 94

Area of Squares and Rectangles 95

Volume of Cubes and Rectangle Prisms 96

Answers of Worksheets – Chapter 11 97

Chapter 12: Three-Dimensional Figures 99

Identify Three–Dimensional Figures 100

Count Vertices, Edges, and Faces 101

Identify Faces of Three–Dimensional Figures 102

Answers of Worksheets – Chapter 12 103

Chapter 13: Symmetry and Transformations 105

Line Segments 106

Identify Lines of Symmetry 107

Count Lines of Symmetry 108

Parallel, Perpendicular and Intersecting Lines 109

Answers of Worksheets – Chapter 13 110

Chapter 14: Fractions 112

Fractions 113

Add Fractions with Like Denominators 114

Subtract Fractions with Like Denominators 115
Add and Subtract Fractions with Like Denominators 116
Compare Sums and Differences of Fractions with Like Denominators 117
Add 3 or More Fractions with Like Denominators 118
Simplifying Fractions 119
Add Fractions with Unlike Denominators 120
Subtract Fractions with Unlike Denominators 121
Add Fractions with Denominators of 10 and 100 122
Add and Subtract Fractions with Denominators of 10, 100, and 1000 123
Answers of Worksheets – Chapter 14 124

Chapter 15: Mixed Numbers 129
Fractions to Mixed Numbers 130
Mixed Numbers to Fractions 131
Add and Subtract Mixed Numbers 132
Answers of Worksheets – Chapter 15 133

Chapter 16: Decimal 135
Decimal Place Value 136
Ordering and Comparing Decimals 137
Decimal Addition 138
Decimal Subtraction 139
Answers of Worksheets – Chapter 16 140

SSAT Lower Level Quantitative Practice Tests 144
SSAT LOWER LEVEL Math Practice Tests Answers and Explanations 169

Chapter 1: Place Vales and Number Sense

Topics that you'll learn in this chapter:

- ✓ Place Values
- ✓ Compare Numbers
- ✓ Numbers in Numbers
- ✓ Rounding
- ✓ Odd or Even

Place Values

Helpful Hints

The value of the place, or position, of a digit in a number. For the number 3,684.26

Millions	Hundred thousands	Ten thousands	Thousands	Hundreds	Tens	Ones	Decimal point	Tenths	Hundredths	Thousandths	Ten-thousandths	Hundred thousandths	Millionths
			3	6	8	4	.	2	6				

Example: In 456, the 5 is in "tens" position.

✎ Write numbers in expanded form.

1) Thirty–five   30 + 5 = 35

2) Sixty–seven   60 + 7 = 67

3) Forty–two   40 + 2 = 42

4) Eighty–nine   80 + 9 = 89

5) Ninety–one   90 + 1 = 91

✎ Circle the correct choice.

6) The 2 in 72 is in the   **(ones place)** tens place   hundreds place

7) The 6 in 65 is in the   ones place   **(tens place)**   hundreds place

8) The 2 in 342 is in the   **(ones place)** tens place   hundreds place

9) The 5 in 450 is in the   ones place   **(tens place)**   hundreds place

10) The 3 in 321 is in the   ones place   tens place   **(hundreds place)**

Comparing and Ordering Numbers

Helpful Hints

Comparing:
Equal to =
Less than <
Greater than >
Greater than or equal ≥
Less than or equal ≤

To compare numbers, you can use number line! As you move from left to right on the number line, you find a bigger number!

Example:

56 > 35

Order integers from least to greatest.
(− 11, − 13, 7, − 2, 12)
− 13 <− 11< − 2 < 7 <12

✎ Use less than, equal to or greater than.

1) 23 < 34
2) 89 __ 98
3) 45 > 25
4) 34 > 32
5) 91 = 91
6) 57 > 55
7) 85 > 78

8) 56 < 43
9) 34 = 34
10) 92 < 98
11) 38 < 46
12) 67 > 58
13) 88 > 69
14) 23 < 34

✎ Order each set numbers from least to greatest.

15) − 15, − 19, 20, − 4, 1   2, 3, 4, 5, 6, __

16) 6, − 5, 4, − 3, 2   ___, ___, ___, ___, ___

17) 15, − 42, 19, 0, − 22   ___, ___, ___, ___, ___

18) 26, − 91, 0, − 13, 67, − 55   ___, ___, ___, ___, ___, ___

19) − 17, − 71, 90, − 25, − 54, − 39   ___, ___, ___, ___, ___, ___

20) 98, 5, 46, 19, 77, 24   ___, ___, ___, ___, ___, ___

Write Numbers in Words

Helpful Hints

- First, learn to write numbers from 1 to 9.
1 = one, 2 = two, 3 = three, 4 = four, 5 = five,
6 = six, 7 = seven, 8 = eight, 9 = nine
- Learn how to write numbers from 10 to 100. For example: 16 = sixteen, 50 = fifty, 89 = eighty-nine
- Learn how to combine words to write more numbers.
For example: 120 is written as: one hundred twenty

✏️ *Write each number in words.*

1) 434   Four, three, four.

2) 809 _____

3) 730 _____

4) 272 _____

5) 266 _____

6) 902 _____

7) 1,418 _____

8) 1,365 _____

9) 3,374 _____

10) 2,486 _____

11) 7,671 _____

12) 6,290 _____

13) 3,147 _____

14) 5,012 _____

Rounding Numbers

| Helpful Hints | Rounding is putting a number up or down to the nearest whole number or the nearest hundred, etc. | **Example:** 64 rounded to the nearest ten is 60, because 64 is closer to 60 than to 70. |

✍ *Round each number to the underlined place value.*

1) 1<u>9</u>72

2) 2,<u>9</u>95

3) 33<u>6</u>4

4) 12<u>8</u>1

5) 23<u>5</u>5

6) 13<u>3</u>4

7) 1,<u>2</u>03

8) 14<u>5</u>7

9) 7<u>4</u>84

10) 19<u>1</u>4

11) 42<u>3</u>9

12) <u>9</u>,123

13) 3,4<u>5</u>2

14) 2<u>5</u>69

15) 1,<u>2</u>30

16) 7<u>6</u>98

17) 92<u>9</u>3

18) 52<u>3</u>7

19) 24<u>9</u>3

20) 2,<u>9</u>23

21) <u>9</u>,845

22) 45<u>5</u>5

23) 6<u>9</u>39

24) 98<u>6</u>9

Odd or Even

Helpful Hints	**Even:** Any integer that can be divided exactly by 2 is an even number. **Odd:** Any integer that cannot be divided exactly by 2 is an odd number.	**Example:** −3, 1, 7 are all odd numbers − 12, 0, 8 are all even numbers

✎ *Identify whether each number is even or odd.*

1) 12 _____

2) 7 _____

3) 33 _____

4) 18 _____

5) 99 _____

6) 55 _____

7) 34 _____

8) 87 _____

9) 94 _____

10) 14 _____

11) 22 _____

12) 79 _____

✎ *Circle the even number in each group.*

13) 22, 11, 57, 13, 19, 47

14) 15, 17, 27, 23, 33, 26

15) 19, 35, 24, 57, 65, 49

16) 67, 58, 89, 63, 27, 63

✎ *Circle the odd number in each group.*

17) 12, 14, 22, 64, 53, 98

18) 16, 26, 28, 44, 62, 73

19) 46, 82, 63, 98, 64, 56

20) 27, 92, 58, 36, 38, 72

Answers of Worksheets – Chapter 1

Place Values

1) 30 + 5
2) 60 + 7
3) 40 + 2
4) 80 + 9
5) 90 + 1
6) ones place
7) tens place
8) ones place
9) tens place
10) hundreds place

Comparing and Ordering Numbers

1) 23 less than 34
2) 89 less than 98
3) 45 greater than 25
4) 34 greater than 32
5) 91 equal to 91
6) 57 greater than 55
7) 85 greater than 78
8) 56 greater than 43
9) 34 equal to 34
10) 92 less than 98
11) 38 less than 46
12) 67 greater than 58
13) 88 greater than 69
14) 23 less than 34
15) −19, −15, −4, 1, 20
16) −5, −3, 2, 4, 6
17) −42, −22, 0, 15, 19
18) −91, −55, −13, 0, 26, 67
19) −71, −54, −39, −25, −17, 90
20) 5, 19, 24, 46, 77, 98

Word Names for Numbers

1) four hundred thirty-four
2) eight hundred nine
3) seven hundred thirty
4) two hundred seventy-two
5) two hundred sixty-six
6) nine hundred two
7) one thousand, four hundred eighteen
8) one thousand, three hundred sixty-five

9) three thousand, three hundred seventy-four

10) two thousand, four hundred eighty-six

11) seven thousand, six hundred seventy-one

12) six thousand, two hundred ninety

13) three thousand, one hundred forty-seven

14) five thousand, twelve

Roman Numerals

1) II
2) VI
3) IV
4) IX
5) X
6) VII
7) III
8) I
9) V
10) VIII
11) IX
12) XI
13) VI
14) XII

Rounding Numbers

1) 2000
2) 3000
3) 3360
4) 1280
5) 2360
6) 1330
7) 1200
8) 1460
9) 7500
10) 1910
11) 4240
12) 9000
13) 3450
14) 2600
15) 1200
16) 7700
17) 9290
18) 5240
19) 2490
20) 2900
21) 10,000
22) 4560
23) 6900
24) 9870

Odd or Even

1) even
2) odd
3) odd
4) even
5) odd
6) odd
7) even
8) odd
9) even
10) even
11) even
12) odd
13) 22
14) 26
15) 24
16) 58
17) 53
18) 73
19) 63
20) 27

Chapter 2: Adding and Subtracting

Topics that you'll learn in this chapter:

- ✓ Adding Two–Digit Numbers
- ✓ Subtracting Two–Digit Numbers
- ✓ Adding Three–Digit Numbers
- ✓ Adding Hundreds
- ✓ Adding 4–Digit Numbers
- ✓ Subtracting 4–Digit Numbers

Adding Two–Digit Numbers

Helpful Hints

1– Line up the numbers.
2– Start with the ones place.
3– Regroup if necessary.
4– Add the tens place.
5– Continue with other digits.

Example:

$$\begin{array}{r} 1,349 \\ +2,411 \\ \hline 3,760 \end{array}$$

✏ Find each sum.

1) $\begin{array}{r} 50 \\ +18 \\ \hline \end{array}$

2) $\begin{array}{r} 32 \\ +14 \\ \hline \end{array}$

3) $\begin{array}{r} 45 \\ +16 \\ \hline \end{array}$

4) $\begin{array}{r} 12 \\ +12 \\ \hline \end{array}$

5) $\begin{array}{r} 43 \\ +30 \\ \hline \end{array}$

6) $\begin{array}{r} 34 \\ +15 \\ \hline \end{array}$

7) $\begin{array}{r} 89 \\ +7 \\ \hline \end{array}$

8) $\begin{array}{r} 63 \\ +12 \\ \hline \end{array}$

9) $\begin{array}{r} 90 \\ +10 \\ \hline \end{array}$

Subtracting Two–Digit Numbers

Helpful Hints

1– Line up the numbers.
2– Start with the units place. (ones place)
3– Regroup if necessary.
4– Subtract the tens place.
5– Continue with other digits.

Example:
$$\begin{array}{r} 5{,}397 \\ -\ 2{,}416 \\ \hline 2{,}981 \end{array}$$

✎ Find each difference.

1) $\begin{array}{r} 32 \\ -15 \\ \hline \end{array}$

2) $\begin{array}{r} 40 \\ -12 \\ \hline \end{array}$

3) $\begin{array}{r} 67 \\ -17 \\ \hline \end{array}$

4) $\begin{array}{r} 18 \\ -10 \\ \hline \end{array}$

5) $\begin{array}{r} 59 \\ -16 \\ \hline \end{array}$

6) $\begin{array}{r} 89 \\ -20 \\ \hline \end{array}$

7) $\begin{array}{r} 78 \\ -21 \\ \hline \end{array}$

8) $\begin{array}{r} 66 \\ -15 \\ \hline \end{array}$

9) $\begin{array}{r} 87 \\ -45 \\ \hline \end{array}$

Adding Three–Digit Numbers

Helpful Hints

1– Line up the numbers.
2– Start with the unit place. (ones place)
3– Regroup if necessary.
4– Add the tens place.
5– Continue with other digits.

Example:
$$\begin{array}{r} 120 \\ +\,114 \\ \hline 234 \end{array}$$

✍ Find each sum.

1) $\begin{array}{r} 234 \\ +\ 56 \\ \hline \end{array}$

2) $\begin{array}{r} 523 \\ +\,134 \\ \hline \end{array}$

3) $\begin{array}{r} 345 \\ +\,167 \\ \hline \end{array}$

4) $\begin{array}{r} 460 \\ +\,120 \\ \hline \end{array}$

5) $\begin{array}{r} 432 \\ +\,430 \\ \hline \end{array}$

6) $\begin{array}{r} 235 \\ +\,150 \\ \hline \end{array}$

7) $\begin{array}{r} 789 \\ +\ 57 \\ \hline \end{array}$

8) $\begin{array}{r} 863 \\ +\,340 \\ \hline \end{array}$

9) $\begin{array}{r} 956 \\ +\ 89 \\ \hline \end{array}$

Adding Hundreds

Helpful Hints

1– Line up the numbers.
2– Start with the ones place.
3– Regroup if necessary.
4– Add the tens place and regroup if necessary.
5– Add the hundred digits.

Example:
$$\begin{array}{r} 500 \\ +\,200 \\ \hline 700 \end{array}$$

✎ Add.

1) 200 + 200 = ——

2) 300 + 200 = ——

3) 500 + 200 = ——

4) 900 + 100 = ——

5) 100 + 700 = ——

6) 500 + 100 = ——

7) 200 + 800 = ——

8) 800 + 100 = ——

9) 700 + 100 = ——

10) 100 + 300 = ——

11) 500 + 500 = ——

12) 400 + 400 = ——

13) 300 + 400 = ——

14) 500 + 300 = ——

15) If there are 600 balls in a box and Jackson puts 500 more balls inside, how many balls are in the box?

_____ balls

Adding 4–Digit Numbers

Helpful *Hints*	1– Line up the numbers. 2– Start with the unit place. (ones place) 3– Regroup if necessary. 4– Add the tens place. 5– Continue with other digits.	Example: $1,349$ $\underline{+2,411}$ $3,760$

✏️ **Add.**

1) $1,158$
   $\underline{+6,687}$

2) $5,188$
   $\underline{+1,298}$

3) $5,756$
   $\underline{+2,712}$

4) $3,239$
   $\underline{+2,562}$

5) $4,257$
   $\underline{+5,194}$

6) $6,215$
   $\underline{+2,189}$

✏️ **Find the missing numbers.**

7) 1,145 + ___ = 1,276

8) 500 + 1,000 = ___

9) 3,200 + ___ = 4,300

10) 455 + ___ = 1,755

11) ___ + 720 = 1,250

12) ___ + 670 = 2,230

13) David sells gems. He finds a diamond in Istanbul and buys it for $3,433. Then, he flies to Cairo and purchases a bigger diamond for the bargain price of $5,922. How much does David spend on the two diamonds?

Subtracting 4–Digit Numbers

Helpful Hints

1– Line up the numbers.
2– Start with the units place. (ones place)
3– Regroup if necessary.
4– Subtract the tens place.
5– Continue with other digits.

Example:
$$\begin{array}{r} 5,397 \\ -2,416 \\ \hline 2,981 \end{array}$$

✏ Subtract.

1) $\begin{array}{r} 8,519 \\ -5,422 \\ \hline \end{array}$

3) $\begin{array}{r} 7,821 \\ -3,212 \\ \hline \end{array}$

5) $\begin{array}{r} 9,290 \\ -3,829 \\ \hline \end{array}$

2) $\begin{array}{r} 6,222 \\ -4,331 \\ \hline \end{array}$

4) $\begin{array}{r} 8,756 \\ -6,712 \\ \hline \end{array}$

6) $\begin{array}{r} 5,117 \\ -4,216 \\ \hline \end{array}$

✏ Find the missing number.

7) 2223 – ___ = 1120

8) 3574 – ___ = 2245

9) 1124 – 578 = ___

10) 2300 – ___ = 1250

11) 3780 – 1890 = ___

12) 2880 – 2560 = ___

13) Jackson had $3,963 invested in the stock market until he lost $2,171 on those investments. How much money does he have in the stock market now?

Answers of Worksheets – Chapter 2

Adding two–digit numbers

1) 68
2) 46
3) 61
4) 24
5) 73
6) 49
7) 96
8) 75
9) 100

Subtracting two–digit numbers

1) 17
2) 28
3) 50
4) 8
5) 43
6) 69
7) 57
8) 51
9) 42

Adding three–digit numbers

1) 290
2) 657
3) 512
4) 580
5) 862
6) 385
7) 846
8) 1,203
9) 1,045

Adding hundreds

1) 400
2) 500
3) 700
4) 1,000
5) 800
6) 600
7) 1,000
8) 900
9) 800
10) 400
11) 1,000
12) 800
13) 700
14) 800
15) 1,100

Adding 4–digit numbers

1) 7,845
2) 6,486
3) 8,468
4) 5,801
5) 9,451
6) 8,404
7) 131
8) 1,500
9) 1,100
10) 1,300
11) 530
12) 1,560
13) $9,355

Subtracting 4–digit numbers

1) 3,097
2) 1,891
3) 4,609
4) 2,044
5) 5,461
6) 901
7) 1,103
8) 1,329
9) 546
10) 1,050
11) 1,890
12) 320
13) 1,792

Chapter 3: Multiplication and Division

Topics that you'll learn in this chapter:

- ✓ Multiplication
- ✓ Division
- ✓ Long Division by One Digit
- ✓ Division with Remainders

Multiplication

> **Helpful Hints**
> – Learn the times tables first!
> – For multiplication, line up the numbers you are multiplying.
> – Start with the ones place.
> – Continue with other digits
>
> **Example:**
> 200 × 90 = 18,000

✏️ Find the answers.

1) 45 × 13

2) 32 × 10

3) 120 × 9

4) 563 × 4

5) 365 × 5

6) 89 × 25

7) 478 × 34

8) 956 × 26

9) 391 × 78

10) The Haunted House Ride runs 5 times a day. It has 6 cars, each of which can hold 4 people. How many people can ride the Haunted House Ride in one day?

11) Each train car has 3 rows of seats. There are 4 seats in each row. How many seats are there in 5 train cars?

Division

> **Helpful Hints**
>
> A typical division problem:
> $$\text{Dividend} \div \text{Divisor} = \text{Quotient}$$
> — In division, we want to find how many times a number (divisor) is contained in another number (dividend).
> — The result in a division problem is the quotient.

✎ **Find each missing number.**

1) $10 \div \underline{} = 1$

2) $48 \div 12 = \underline{}$

3) $99 \div \underline{} = 9$

4) $70 \div 10 = \underline{}$

5) $44 \div \underline{} = 4$

6) $24 \div \underline{} = 2$

7) $\underline{} \div 10 = 4$

8) $110 \div 11 = \underline{}$

9) $12 \div \underline{} = 1$

10) $90 \div \underline{} = 9$

11) $\underline{} \div 11 = 8$

12) $\underline{} \div 12 = 11$

13) $60 \div \underline{} = 6$

14) $\underline{} \div 11 = 12$

15) $84 \div 12 = \underline{}$

16) $80 \div 10 = \underline{}$

17) $11 \div 11 = \underline{}$

18) $144 \div \underline{} = 12$

19) Anna has 120 books. She wants to put them in equal numbers on 12 bookshelves. How many books can she put on a bookshelf? _____ books

20) If dividend is 99 and the quotient is 11, then what is the divisor? _____

Long Division by One Digit

Helpful Hints
- Remember that long division moves from left to right.
- Begin with the number in the left side. (If the dividend is a 3-digit numbers, begin with hundreds place.)
- If the first digit of dividend is smaller than the divisor, choose another digit from dividend.

✎ *Find the quotient.*

1) $6\overline{)792}$

2) $5\overline{)350}$

3) $6\overline{)174}$

4) $8\overline{)104}$

5) $3\overline{)102}$

6) $9\overline{)189}$

7) $5\overline{)115}$

8) $2\overline{)120}$

9) $7\overline{)112}$

10) $4\overline{)148}$

11) $9\overline{)126}$

12) $6\overline{)240}$

13) $4\overline{)576}$

14) $4\overline{)512}$

15) $9\overline{)1278}$

16) $8\overline{)2768}$

17) $6\overline{)1224}$

18) $4\overline{)3412}$

Division with Remainders

Helpful Hints
- Set up the division problem with the long division bracket.
- Divide the first digit of the dividend by the divisor.
- Write the answer on top of the division bracket.
- Continue with other digits of the dividend.
- Continue the process until the remainder is smaller than the divisor.

✎ *Find the quotient with remainder.*

1) $5\overline{)592}$

2) $3\overline{)295}$

3) $6\overline{)553}$

4) $5\overline{)214}$

5) $3\overline{)440}$

6) $7\overline{)673}$

7) $4\overline{)213}$

8) $2\overline{)820}$

9) $5\overline{)496}$

10) $6\overline{)791}$

11) $4\overline{)647}$

12) $7\overline{)780}$

13) $4\overline{)5910}$

14) $8\overline{)3515}$

15) $7\overline{)2355}$

16) $9\overline{)1232}$

17) $8\overline{)6029}$

18) $4\overline{)6743}$

Answers of Worksheets – Chapter 3

Multiplication

1) 585
2) 320
3) 1,080
4) 2,252
5) 1,825
6) 2,225
7) 16,252
8) 24,856
9) 30,498
10) 120
11) 60

Division

1) 10
2) 4
3) 11
4) 7
5) 11
6) 12
7) 40
8) 10
9) 12
10) 10
11) 88
12) 132
13) 10
14) 132
15) 7
16) 8
17) 1
18) 12
19) 10
20) 9

Long Division by One Digit

1) 132
2) 70
3) 29
4) 13
5) 34
6) 21
7) 23
8) 60
9) 16
10) 37
11) 14
12) 40
13) 144
14) 128
15) 142
16) 346
17) 204
18) 853

Division with Remainders

1) 118 R4
2) 98 R1
3) 92 R1
4) 42 R4
5) 146 R2
6) 96 R1
7) 53 R1
8) 410 R0
9) 99 R1
10) 131 R5
11) 161 R3
12) 111 R3
13) 1477 R2
14) 439 R3
15) 336 R3
16) 135 R8
17) 753 R5
18) 1685 R3

Chapter 4: Mixed operations

Topics that you'll learn in this chapter:

- ✓ Rounding and Estimating
- ✓ Estimate Sums
- ✓ Estimate Differences
- ✓ Estimate Products
- ✓ Missing Numbers

Rounding and Estimating

Helpful Hints

– Rounding is putting a number up or down to the nearest whole number or the nearest hundred, etc.
– To estimate means to make a rough guess or calculation.
– To round means to simplify a number by scaling it slightly up or down.

Example:
64 rounded to the nearest ten is 60, because 64 is closer to 60 than to 70.

Estimate:
73 + 69 ≈ 70 + 70 = 140

✏ Round each number to the underlined place value.

1) 9<u>7</u>2

2) 2,<u>9</u>95

3) 3<u>6</u>4

4) <u>8</u>1

5) <u>5</u>5

6) 3<u>3</u>4

7) 1,<u>2</u>03

8) 9.<u>5</u>7

9) 7.<u>4</u>84

✏ Estimate the sum by rounding each added to the nearest ten.

10) 55 + 9

11) 13 + 74

12) 83 + 7

13) 32 + 37

14) 13 + 74

15) 34 + 11

16) 39 + 77

17) 25 + 4

18) 61 + 73

19) 64 + 59

20) 14 + 68

21) 82 + 12

22) 43 + 66

23) 45 + 65

24) 553 + 232

Estimate Sums

> **Helpful Hints**
>
> – To estimate means to make a rough guess or calculation.
> – For addition, you can round numbers and then solve the problems.
>
> **Example:**
> 54 + 26 = 50 + 30 = 80

✏️ *Estimate the sum by rounding each added to the nearest ten.*

1) 55 + 9

2) 13 + 74

3) 83 + 7

4) 32 + 37

5) 13 + 74

6) 34 + 11

7) 39 + 77

8) 25 + 4

9) 61 + 73

10) 64 + 59

11) 14 + 68

12) 82 + 12

13) 43 + 66

14) 45 + 65

15) 553 + 232

16) 52 + 67

17) 96 + 94

18) 29 + 89

19) 78 + 74

20) 39 + 27

21) 91 + 68

22) 48 + 81

23) 14 + 96

24) 52 + 59

Estimate Differences

Helpful Hints

− To estimate means to make a rough guess or calculation.
− For subtraction, you can round numbers and then solve the problems.

Example:
37 − 12 = 40 − 10 = 30

✏️ *Estimate the difference by rounding each number to the nearest ten.*

1) 46 − 11

2) 23 − 14

3) 68 − 36

4) 22 − 13

5) 59 − 36

6) 34 − 11

7) 67 − 37

8) 38 − 19

9) 84 − 38

10) 68 − 48

11) 58 − 16

12) 72 − 27

13) 63 − 33

14) 49 − 32

15) 94 − 63

16) 55 − 32

17) 87 − 74

18) 32 − 11

19) 46 − 39

20) 99 − 36

21) 94 − 78

22) 75 − 23

23) 99 − 19

24) 86 − 43

Estimate Products

> **Helpful Hints**
>
> – To estimate means to make a rough guess or calculation.
> – You can round numbers to estimate the result.
>
> Example:
> **44** × 17 = 40 × 20 = 800

✎ *Estimate the products.*

1) 27 × 18

2) 13 × 17

3) 22 × 25

4) 43 × 19

5) 68 × 23

6) 36 × 91

7) 53 × 92

8) 18 × 38

9) 21 × 14

10) 83 × 42

11) 51 × 32

12) 68 × 12

13) 47 × 23

14) 71 × 58

15) 54 × 89

16) 37 × 72

17) 36 × 93

18) 32 × 29

19) 41 × 37

20) 54 × 93

21) 89 × 72

22) 77 × 22

23) 53 × 13

24) 98 × 63

Missing Numbers

Helpful Hints
- To find the missing factors in multiplication, you can sometimes use division rule.
- Remember, multiplication and division are opposite operations!

Example:

___ × 5 = 45

To solve this problem, simply divide 45 by 5. The answer is 9.

✏️ Find the missing numbers.

1) 20 × ___ = 60

2) 16 × ___ = 32

3) ___ × 14 = 84

4) 16 × ___ = 80

5) ___ × 19 = 38

6) 17 × ___ = 34

7) ___ × 1 = 18

8) 21 × ___ = 42

9) 20 × ___ = 80

10) 15 × 7 = ___

11) 18 × 9 = ___

12) 21 × 4 = ___

13) 23 × 7 = ___

14) ___ × 25 = 75

15) 24 × ___ = 120

16) 22 × 4 = ___

17) 20 × ___ = 140

18) 17 × ___ = 153

19) ___ × 15 = 120

20) 21 × 6 = ___

21) ___ × 22 = 154

22) 19 × ___ = 76

23) 23 × 9 = ___

24) 25 × 6 = ___

25) ___ × 18 = 36

26) 24 × ___ = 48

Answers of Worksheets – Chapter 4

Rounding and Estimating

1) 1,000
2) 3,000
3) 360
4) 80
5) 60
6) 330
7) 1,200
8) 9.6
9) 7.5
10) 70
11) 80
12) 90
13) 70
14) 80
15) 40
16) 120
17) 30
18) 130
19) 120
20) 80
21) 90
22) 110
23) 120
24) 780

Estimate sums

1) 70
2) 80
3) 90
4) 70
5) 80
6) 40
7) 120
8) 30
9) 130
10) 120
11) 80
12) 90
13) 110
14) 120
15) 780
16) 120
17) 190
18) 120
19) 150
20) 70
21) 160
22) 130
23) 110
24) 110

Estimate differences

1) 40
2) 10
3) 30
4) 10
5) 20
6) 20
7) 30
8) 20
9) 40
10) 20
11) 40
12) 40
13) 30
14) 20
15) 30
16) 30
17) 20
18) 20
19) 10
20) 60
21) 10
22) 60
23) 80
24) 50

Estimate products

1) 600
2) 200
3) 600
4) 800
5) 1400
6) 3600
7) 4500
8) 800
9) 200
10) 3200
11) 1500
12) 700
13) 1000
14) 4200
15) 4500
16) 2800
17) 3600
18) 900
19) 1600
20) 4500
21) 6300
22) 1600
23) 500
24) 6000

Missing Numbers

1) 3
2) 2
3) 6
4) 5
5) 2
6) 2
7) 18
8) 2
9) 4
10) 105
11) 162
12) 84
13) 161
14) 3
15) 5
16) 88
17) 7
18) 9
19) 8
20) 126
21) 7
22) 4
23) 207
24) 150
25) 2
26) 2

Chapter 5: Algebra

Topics that you'll learn in this chapter:

- ✓ Evaluating Variable
- ✓ Evaluating Two Variables
- ✓ Solve Equations

Evaluating Variable

Helpful Hints
- To evaluate one variable expression, find the variable and substitute a number for that variable.
- Perform the arithmetic operations.

Example:
$4x + 8, x = 6$
$4(6) + 8 = 24 + 8 = 32$

✎ *Simplify each algebraic expression.*

1) $9 - x$, $x = 3$

2) $x + 2$, $x = 5$

3) $3x + 7$, $x = 6$

4) $x + (-5)$, $x = -2$

5) $3x + 6$, $x = 4$

6) $4x + 6$, $x = -1$

7) $10 + 2x - 6$, $x = 3$

8) $10 - 3x$, $x = 8$

9) $\dfrac{20}{x} - 3$, $x = 5$

10) $(-3) + \dfrac{x}{4} + 2x$, $x = 16$

11) $(-2) + \dfrac{x}{7}$, $x = 21$

12) $(-\dfrac{14}{x}) - 9 + 4x$, $x = 2$

13) $(-\dfrac{6}{x}) - 9 + 2x$, $x = 3$

14) $(-2) + \dfrac{x}{8}$, $x = 16$

15) $8(5x - 12)$, $x = -2$

Evaluating Two Variables

Helpful Hints

To evaluate an algebraic expression, substitute a number for each variable and perform the arithmetic operations.

Example:

$2x + 4y - 3 + 2,$

$x = 5, y = 3$

$2(5) + 4(3) - 3 + 2$
$= 10 + 12 - 3 + 2$
$= 21$

✎ *Simplify each algebraic expression.*

1) $2x + 4y - 3 + 2,$
   $x = 5, y = 3$

2) $(-\dfrac{12}{x}) + 1 + 5y,$
   $x = 6, y = 8$

3) $(-4)(-2a - 2b),$
   $a = 5, b = 3$

4) $10 + 3x + 7 - 2y,$
   $x = 7, y = 6$

5) $9x + 2 - 4y,$
   $x = 7, y = 5$

6) $6 + 3(-2x - 3y),$
   $x = 9, y = 7$

7) $12x + y,$
   $x = 4, y = 8$

8) $x \times 4 \div y,$
   $x = 3, y = 2$

9) $2x + 14 + 4y,$
   $x = 6, y = 8$

10) $4a - (5 - b),$
    $a = 4, b = 6$

Solve Equations

> **Helpful Hints**
>
> - The values of two expressions on both sides of an equation are equal.
> $$ax + b = c$$
> - You only need to perform one Math operation in order to solve the equation.
>
> Example:
>
> $-8x = 16$
>
> $x = -2$

✎ Solve each equation.

1) $x + 3 = 17$

2) $22 = (-8) + x$

3) $3x = (-30)$

4) $(-36) = (-6x)$

5) $(-6) = 4 + x$

6) $2 + x = (-2)$

7) $20x = (-220)$

8) $18 = x + 5$

9) $(-23) + x = (-19)$

10) $5x = (-45)$

11) $x - 12 = (-25)$

12) $x - 3 = (-12)$

13) $(-35) = x - 27$

14) $8 = 2x$

15) $(-6x) = 36$

16) $(-55) = (-5x)$

17) $x - 30 = 20$

18) $8x = 32$

19) $36 = (-4x)$

20) $4x = 68$

21) $30x = 300$

Answers of Worksheets – Chapter 5

Evaluating Variable

1) 6
2) 7
3) 25
4) −7
5) 18
6) 2
7) 10
8) −14
9) 1
10) 33
11) 1
12) −8
13) −5
14) 0
15) −176

Evaluating Two Variables

1) 21
2) 39
3) 64
4) 26
5) 45
6) −111
7) 56
8) 6
9) 58
10) 17

Solve Equations

1) 14
2) 30
3) − 10
4) 6
5) − 10
6) − 4
7) − 11
8) 13
9) 4
10) − 9
11) − 13
12) − 9
13) − 8
14) 4
15) − 6
16) 11
17) 50
18) 4
19) − 9
20) 17
21) 10

Chapter 6: Data and Graphs

Topics that you'll learn in this chapter:

- ✓ Graph Points on a Coordinate Plane
- ✓ Bar Graph
- ✓ Tally and Pictographs
- ✓ Line Graphs
- ✓ Stem–And–Leaf Plot
- ✓ Scatter Plots

Graph Points on a Coordinate Plane

Helpful Hints

- Understand the axes of the coordinate plane:
x-axis goes left and right and y-axis goes up and down.
- You should graph the point in (x, y) form.
- Start at (0, 0).
- Move over x unit to the right if x is positive and move to left if it's negative.
- Move over y units up (if it is positive) or down (if it is negative).

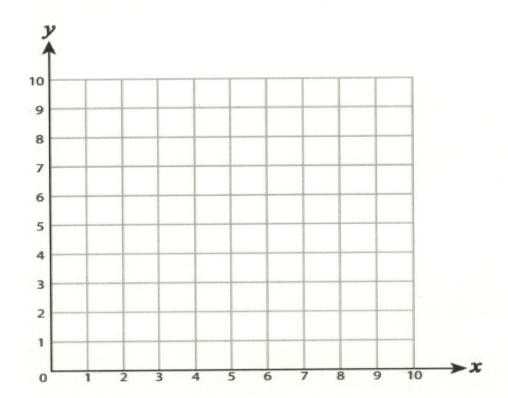

Plot each point on the coordinate grid.

1) A (3, 6)

2) B (1, 3)

3) C (3, 7)

4) D (8, 6)

5) E (5, 2)

6) F (9, 3)

Bar Graph

Helpful Hints — A bar graph is a chart that presents data with bars in different heights to match with the values of the data. The bars can be graphed horizontally or vertically.

✎ Graph the given information as a bar graph.

Day	Hot dogs sold
Monday	90
Tuesday	70
Wednesday	30
Thursday	20
Friday	60

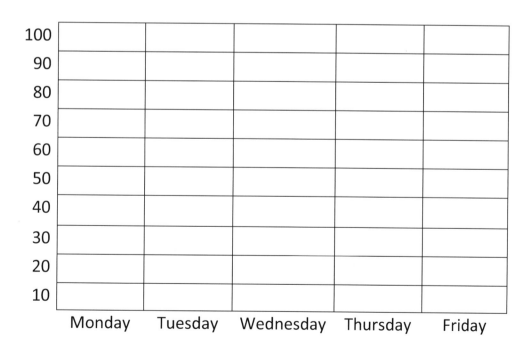

Tally and Pictographs

Helpful Hints
- A pictograph is a picture graph. It is a graph that represents data using symbols.
- To complete a pictograph, first look at the pictures to determine how many items are represented by each symbol.

✎ *Using the key, draw the pictograph to show the information.*

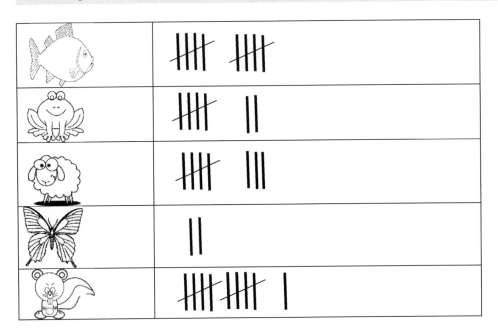

Key: 😊 = 2 animals

Line Graphs

Helpful Hints
- Line graphs represent how something changes over time.
- There are two arises in a line graph, x-axis is the horizontal line and y-axis is vertical.
- x-axis is usually used to show time period and the y-axis shows numbers for what is being represented.

✏️ *David work as a salesman in a store. He records the number of shoes sold in five days on a line graph. Use the graph to answer the questions.*

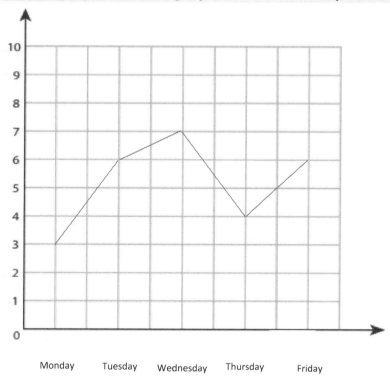

1) How many cars were sold on Monday?

2) Which day had the minimum sales of shoes?

3) Which day had the maximum number of shoes sold?

4) How many shoes were sold in 5 days?

Stem–And–Leaf Plot

> **Helpful Hints**
> – Stem–and–leaf plots display the frequency of the values in a data set.
> – We can make a frequency distribution table for the values, or we can use a stem–and–leaf plot.

Example:

56, 58, 42, 48, 66, 64, 53, 69, 45, 72

Stem	leaf
4	2 5 8
5	3 6 8
6	4 6 9
7	2

✎ *Make stem ad leaf plots for the given data.*

1) 74, 88, 97, 72, 79, 86, 95, 79, 83, 91

2) 37, 48, 26, 33, 49, 26, 19, 26, 48

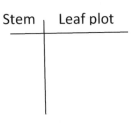

3) 58, 41, 42, 67, 54, 65, 65, 54, 69, 53

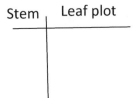

Scatter Plots

> **Helpful Hints**
>
> A Scatter (xy) Plot shows the values with points that represent the relationship between two sets of data.
>
> − The horizontal values are usually x and vertical data is y.

✎ **Construct a scatter plot.**

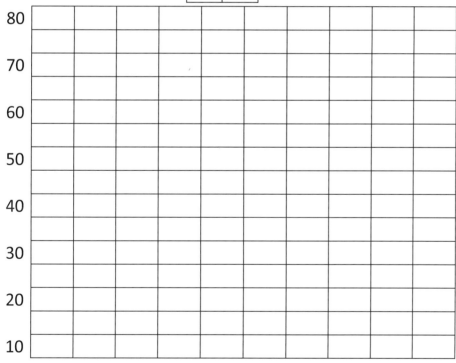

X	Y
1	20
2	40
3	50
4	60

Answers of Worksheets – Chapter 6

Graph Points on a Coordinate Plane

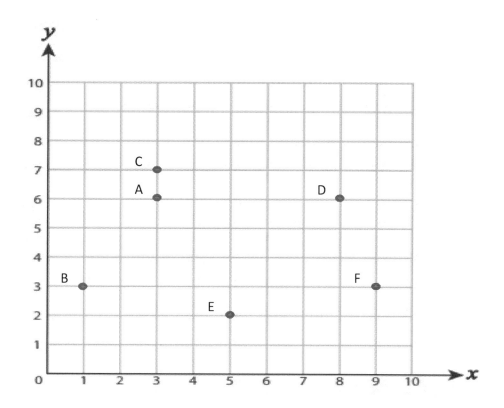

Bar Graph

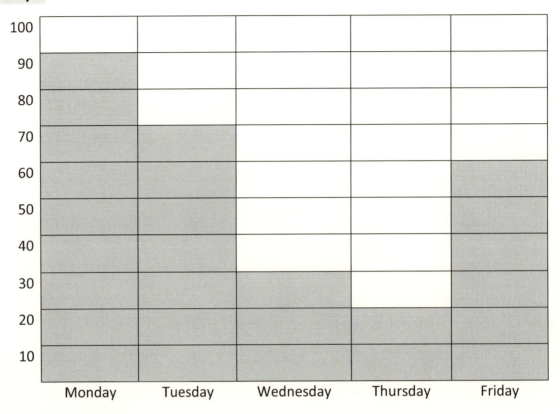

Tally and Pictographs

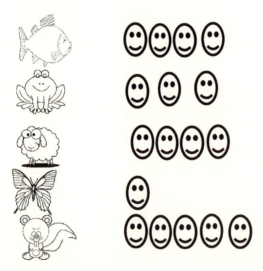

Line Graphs

1) 3

2) Thursday

3) Wednesday

4) 26

Stem–And–Leaf Plot

1)

Stem	leaf
7	2 4 9 9
8	3 6 8
9	1 5 7

2)

Stem	leaf
1	9
2	6 6 6
3	3 7
4	8 8 9

3)

Stem	leaf
4	1 2
5	3 4 4 8
6	5 5 7 9

Scatter Plots

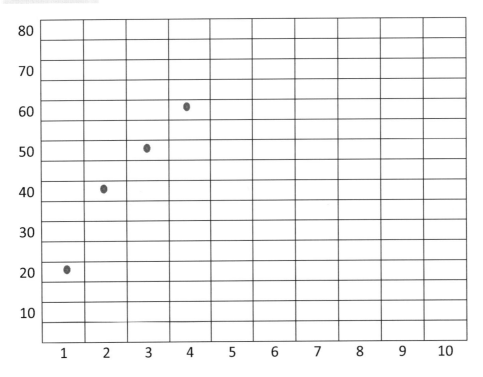

Chapter 7: Patterns and Sequences

Topics that you'll learn in this chapter:

- ✓ Repeating pattern
- ✓ Growing Patterns
- ✓ Patterns: Numbers
- ✓ Patterns

Repeating Pattern

> **Helpful Hints**
> - Look for a relationship between two shapes in a row.
> - After finding the rule, check the pattern for all other shapes.
> - Use the rule to find next shapes.
>
> Example:

✎ *Circle the picture that comes next in each picture pattern.*

1)

2)

3)

4)

Growing Patterns

Helpful Hints
- Look for a relationship between two shapes in a row.
- After finding the rule, check the pattern for all other shapes.
- Use the rule to find next shapes.

✏️ Draw the picture that comes next in each growing pattern.

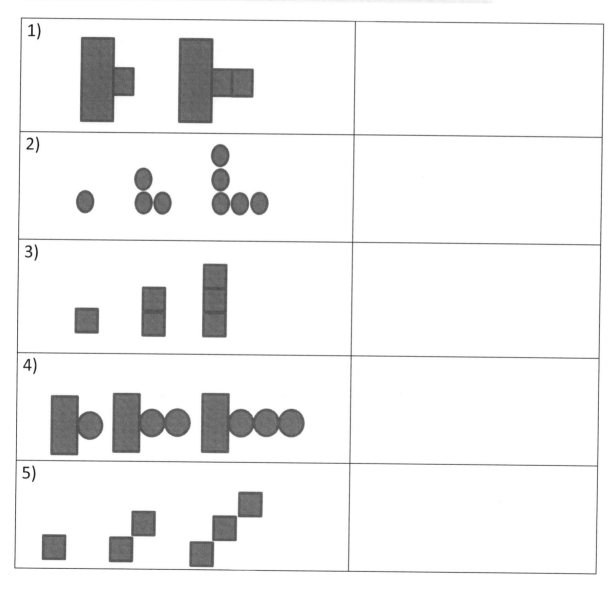

Patterns: Numbers

> **Helpful Hints**
> - Look for a relationship between two numbers in a row.
> - After finding the rule, check the pattern for all other numbers.
> - Use the rule to find next numbers.
>
> **Example:**
> 2, 5, 8, 11, 14, ...
>
> Rule: The number + 3
>
> 2, 5, 8, 11, 14, 17, 20, 23

✍ *Write the numbers that come next.*

1) 3, 6, 9, 12,   ____, ____, ____, ____

2) 2, 4, 6, 8,   ____, ____, ____, ____

3) 5, 10, 15, 20,   ____, ____, ____, ____

4) 15, 25, 35, 45,   ____, ____, ____, ____

5) 11, 22, 33, 44,   ____, ____, ____, ____

6) 10, 18, 26, 34, 42,   ____, ____, ____, ____

7) 61, 55, 49, 43, 37,   ____, ____, ____, ____

8) 45, 56, 67, 78,   ____, ____, ____, ____

9) 3, 6, 9, 12, 15, 18, 21, 24   ____, ____, ____, ____

Patterns

Helpful Hints
- A pattern is a group of numbers or objects that follow a rule.
- There is a rule in any pattern for repeating and changing.

✍ **Write the next three numbers in each counting sequence.**

1) −32, −23, −14, _____, _____, _____, _____

2) 543, 528, 513, _____, _____, _____, _____

3) _____, _____, 56, 64, _____, 80

4) 23, 34, _____, _____, 67, _____

5) 24, 31, _____, _____, _____

6) 52, 45, _____, _____, _____

7) 51, 44, 37, _____, _____, _____

8) 64, 51, 38, _____, _____, _____

9) What are the next three numbers in this counting sequence?

   1350, 1550, 1750, _____, _____, _____

10) What is the seventh number in this counting sequence?

   7, 16, 25, _____

Answers of Worksheets – Chapter 7

Repeating pattern

1)

2)

3)

4)

Growing patterns

1)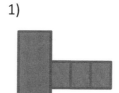

2)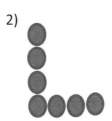

3)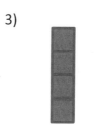

4)

5)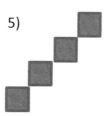

Patterns: Numbers

1) 3, 6, 9, 12, 15, 18, 21, 24
2) 2, 4, 6, 8, 10, 12, 14, 16
3) 5, 10, 15, 20, 25, 30, 35, 40
4) 15, 25, 35, 45, 55, 65, 75, 85
5) 11, 22, 33, 44, 55, 66, 77, 88
6) 10, 18, 26, 34, 42, 50, 58, 66
7) 61, 55, 49, 43, 37, 31, 25, 19
8) 45, 56, 67, 78, 89, 100, 111, 122

Patterns

1) –5, 4, 13, 22
2) 498, 483, 468
3) 40–48–56–64–72–80
4) 23–34–45–56–67–78
5) 38–45–52
6) 38–31–24
7) 30, 23, 16
8) 25, 12, –1
9) 1950–2150–2350
10) 61

Chapter 8: Money

Topics that you'll learn in this chapter:

- ✓ Add Money Amounts
- ✓ Subtract Money Amounts
- ✓ Money: Word Problems

Add Money Amounts

Helpful Hints

Example:
$12.23
+$26.55
$38.78

✏ *Subtract.*

1) $314 + $152 　　　 $624 + $410 　　　 $390 + $215

2) $321 + $430 　　　 $530 + $321 　　　 $712 + $145

3) $411 + $316 　　　 $559 + $228 　　　 $731 + $213

4) $621 + $168 　　　 $321 + $129 　　　 $615 + $371

Subtract Money Amounts

Helpful Hints	- For subtracting money, start with the cents and then the dollars. - Move from right to left. - Borrow if it's necessary!	**Example:** $87.47 −$26.44 $61.03

✎ Subtract.

5) $825 $651 $754
   −$166   −$110   −$565
   _____   _____   _____

6) $539 $498 $992
   −$137   −$359   −$549
   _____   _____   _____

7) $436 $512 $632
   −$219   −$128   −$444
   _____   _____   _____

8) Linda had $12.00. She bought some game tickets for $7.14. How much did she have left?

Money: Word Problems

> **Helpful Hints**
>
> - First review key words in word problems and what they mean.
> **Addition:** total, in all, together, and, more than, sum, etc.
> **Subtraction:** difference, less than, minus, left over, etc.
> **Multiplication:** times, product, each, double, etc.
> **Division:** split, row, half, fourth, etc.
>
> **Example:** Peter has 211 blue marbles and 29 red marbles. How many marbles does he have **in all**? (Add 211 + 29 = 240 cards).

✎ Solve.

1) How many boxes of envelopes can you buy with $18 if one box costs $3?

2) After paying $6.25 for a salad, Ella has $45.56. How much money did she have before buying the salad?

3) How many packages of diapers can you buy with $50 if one package costs $5?

4) Last week James ran 20 miles more than Michael. James ran 56 miles. How many miles did Michael run?

5) Last Friday Jacob had $32.52. Over the weekend he received some money for cleaning the attic. He now has $44. How much money did he receive?

6) After paying $10.12 for a sandwich, Amelia has $35.50. How much money did she have before buying the sandwich?

Answers of Worksheets – Chapter 8

Add Money Amounts

1) 466, 1,034, 605
2) 751, 851, 857
3) 727, 787, 944
4) 789, 450, 986

Subtract Money Amounts

1) 659–541–189
2) 402–139–443
3) 217–384–188
4) 4.86

Money: word problem

1) 6
2) $51.81
3) 10
4) 36
5) 11.48
6) 45.62

Chapter 9: Measurement

Topics that you'll learn in this chapter:

- ✓ Metric System
- ✓ Length
- ✓ Temperature
- ✓ Liters & Milliliters
- ✓ Kilograms & Grams

Metric System

Helpful Hints

1 m = 100 cm
1 cm = 10 mm
1 m = 1000 mm
1 km = 1000 m

Example:

12 cm = 0.12 m

✎ **Convert to the units.**

1) 4 mm = _____ cm

2) 0.6 m = _____ mm

3) 2 m = _____ cm

4) 0.03 km = _____ m

5) 3000 mm = _____ km

6) 5 cm _____ m

7) 0.03 m = _____ cm

8) 1000 mm = _____ km

9) 600 mm = _____ m

10) 0.77 km = _____ mm

11) 0.08 km = _____ m

12) 0.30 m = _____ cm

13) 400 m = _____ km

14) 5000 cm = _____ km

15) 40 mm = _____ cm

16) 800 m = _____ km

Length

Helpful Hints	1 foot = 12 inches 1 yard = 3 feet 1 meter = 100 centimeters 1 kilometer = 1000 meters	Example: 3 meter = 300 cm

✎ **Use a ruler to find the length of the line segment below to the nearest quarter inch.**

_____

_____

_____

✎ **Convert the following measurements.**

1) 2 feet = ____ inches

2) 5 feet = ____ inches

3) 1 yard = ____ feet

4) 3 yards = ____ feet

5) 1 meter = ____ centimeter

6) 3 kilometers = ____ meters

7) 100 meters = ____ centimeters

8) 8 yards = ____ feet

Temperature

Helpful Hints	- **Convert Celsius to Fahrenheit:** Multiply the temperature by 1.8 and then add 32 to the result - **Convert Fahrenheit to Celsius:** Subtract 32 from the number and then divide the result by 1.8	Example: 32 °F = 0 °C 10.00 °C = 50 °F

1) ✏ *What temperature is shown on this Celsius thermometer?*

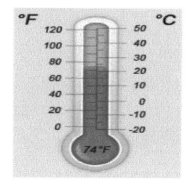

✏ *Convert Celsius into Fahrenheit.*

2) 10°C = ___ °F   6) 25°C = ___ °F   11) 30°C = ___ °F

3) 35°C = ___ °F   8) 50°C = ___ °F   12) 20°C = ___ °F

4) 80°C = ___ °F   9) 45°C = ___ °F   7) 70°C = ___ °F

5) 15°C = ___ °F   10) 90°C = ___ °F   13) 80°C = ___ °F

Liters & Milliliters

Helpful Hints

1 L = 1000 ml

✎ Solve.

1) 10 l = _____ ml

2) 4 l = _____ ml

3) 20 l = _____ ml

4) 24 l = _____ ml

5) 27 l = _____ ml

6) 14 l = _____ ml

7) 50 l = _____ ml

8) 45 l = _____ ml

9) 98 l = _____ ml

10) 1000 ml = _____ l

11) 3000 ml = _____ l

12) 70, 000 ml = _____ l

13) 6000 ml = _____ l

14) 13, 000 ml = _____ l

15) 8000 ml = _____ l

16) 30, 000 ml = _____ l

17) 9000 ml = _____ l

18) 10, 000 ml = _____ l

Kilograms & Grams

> **Helpful Hints**
>
> 1 kg = 1000 g

✎ Solve.

1) 10 kg = _____ g

2) 33 kg = _____ g

3) 100 kg = _____ g

4) 60 kg = _____ g

5) 85 kg = _____ g

6) 120 kg = _____ g

7) 28 kg = _____ g

8) 72 kg = _____ g

9) 56 kg = _____ g

10) 100,000 g = _____ kg

11) 30,000 g = _____ kg

12) 70,000 g = _____ kg

13) 600,000 g = _____ kg

14) 130,000 g = _____ kg

15) 80,000 g = _____ kg

16) 300,000 g = _____ kg

17) 90,000 g = _____ kg

18) 10,000 g = _____ kg

Answers of Worksheets – Chapter 9

Metric System

1) 4 mm = 0.4 cm
2) 0.6 m = 600 mm
3) 2 m = 200 cm
4) 0.03 km = 30 m
5) 3000 mm = 0.003 km
6) 5 cm = 0.05 m
7) 0.03 m = 3 cm
8) 1000 mm = 0.001 km
9) 600 mm = 0.6 m
10) 0.77 km = 770,000 mm
11) 0.08 km = 80 m
12) 0.30 m = 30 cm
13) 400 m = 0.4 km
14) 5000 cm = 0.05 km
15) 40 mm = 4 cm
16) 800 m = 0.8 km

Length

1) 24
2) 60
3) 3
4) 9
5) 100
6) 3000
7) 10000
8) 24

Temperature

1) 20
2) 50
3) 95
4) 176
5) 59
6) 77
7) 122
8) 113
9) 194
10) 86
11) 68
12) 158
13) 176

Liters & Milliliters

1) 10 l = 10,000 ml
2) 4 l = 4,000 ml
3) 20 l = 20,000 ml
4) 24 l = 24,000 ml
5) 27 l = 27,000 ml
6) 14 l = 14,000 ml
7) 50 l = 50,000 ml
8) 45 l = 45,000 ml
9) 98 l = 98,000 ml
10) 1,000 ml = 1 L
11) 3,000 ml = 3 L
12) 70,000 ml = 70 L
13) 6,000 ml = 6 L
14) 13,000 ml = 13 L
15) 8,000 ml = 8 L
16) 30,000 ml = 30 L
17) 9,000 ml = 9 L
18) 10,000 ml = 10 L

Kilograms & Grams

1) 10 kg = 10,000 g
2) 33 kg = 33,000 g
3) 100 kg = 100,000 g
4) 60 kg = 60,000 g
5) 85 kg = 85,000 g
6) 120 kg = 120,000 g
7) 28 kg = 28,000 g
8) 72 kg = 72,000 g
9) 56 kg = 56,000 g
10) 100,000 g = 100 kg
11) 30,000 g = 30 kg
12) 70, 000 g = 70 kg
13) 600,000 g = 600 kg
14) 130,000 g = 130 kg
15) 80,000 g = 80 kg
16) 300,000 g = 300 kg
17) 90,000 g = 90 kg
18) 10,000 g = 10 kg

Chapter 10: Time

Topics that you'll learn in this chapter:

- ✓ Read Clocks
- ✓ Telling Time
- ✓ Digital Clock
- ✓ Measurement – Time

Read Clocks

Helpful Hints
- A clock has a round face with the numbers 1 through 12 on it.
- It has an hour hand and a minute hand to show the hour and minute.
- To tell the hour, look at the number that the short hand just passed.
- To tell the minute, look at the number the longer hand just passed.

✏️ *Write the time below each clock.*

1)

2)

3)

4)

5)

6)

Telling Time

Helpful Hints
- A clock has a round face with the numbers 1 through 12 on it.
- It has an hour hand and a minute hand to show the hour and minute.
- To tell the hour, look at the number that the short hand just passed.
- To tell the minute, look at the number the longer hand just passed.

1) What time is shown by this clock?

   _____

2) It is night. What time is shown on this clock?

   _____

✎ **How much time has passed?**

3) From 1:15 AM to 4:35 AM: _____ hours and _____ minutes.

4) From 1:25 AM to 4:05 AM: _____ hours and _____ minutes.

5) It's 8:30 P.M. What time was 5 hours ago?

   _____ O'clock

Digital Clock

Helpful Hints	- A digital clock contains two numbers separated by a colon. The first number marks the hour and the second number, found after the colon, shows the minutes. - For example, "3 : 14" means the time is "three-fourteen" or "fourteen past three."

✎ What time is it? Write the time in words in front of each.

1) 2 : 30 _____

2) 3 : 15 _____

3) 5 : 45 _____

4) 9 : 20 _____

5) 10 : 5 _____

6) 12 : 50 _____

Measurement – Time

> **Helpful Hints**
>
> 60 minutes = 1 hour
> 60 seconds = 1 minute
>
> Example:
>
> 4 hours = 240 minutes

✎ **How much time has passed?**

1) 1:15 AM to 4:35 AM: _____ hours and _____ minutes.

2) 2:35 AM to 5:10 AM: _____ hours and _____ minutes.

3) 6:00 AM. to 7:25 AM. = _____ hour(s) and _____ minutes.

4) 6:15 PM to 7:30 PM. = _____ hour(s) and _____ minutes

5) 5:15 A.M. to 5:45 A.M. = _____ minutes

6) 4:05 A.M. to 4:30 A.M. = _____ minutes

7) There are _____ second in 15 minutes.

8) There are _____ second in 11 minutes.

9) There are _____ second in 27 minutes.

10) There are _____ minutes in 10 hours.

11) There are _____ minutes in 20 hours.

12) There are _____ minutes in 12 hours.

Answers of Worksheets – Chapter 10

Read clocks

1) 1
2) 4 : 45
3) 8
4) 3 : 30
5) 10 : 15
6) 8 : 35

Telling Time

1) 12:00
2) 22:10 PM
3) 3 hours and 20 minutes
4) 2 hours and 40 minutes
5) 3:30 PM

Digital Clock

1) It's two thirty.
2) It's three Fifteen.
3) It's five forty–five.
4) It's nine twenty.
5) It's ten five.
6) It's Twelve Fifty.

Measurement – Time

1) 3:20
2) 2:35
3) 1:25
4) 1:15
5) 30 minutes
6) 25 minutes
7) 900
8) 660
9) 1,620
10) 600
11) 1,200
12) 720

Chapter 11: Geometric

Topics that you'll learn in this chapter:

- ✓ Identifying Angles: Acute, Right, Obtuse, and Straight Angles
- ✓ Polygon Names
- ✓ Classify Triangles
- ✓ Parallel Sides in Quadrilaterals
- ✓ Identify Rectangles
- ✓ Perimeter: Find the Missing Side Lengths
- ✓ Perimeter and Area of Squares
- ✓ Perimeter and Area of rectangles
- ✓ Find the Area or Missing Side Length of a Rectangle
- ✓ Area and Perimeter: Word Problems
- ✓ Area of Squares and Rectangles
- ✓ Volume of Cubes and Rectangle Prisms

Identifying Angles: Acute, Right, Obtuse, and Straight Angles

Helpful	Angle Type	Measure Range
	acute	0° to 90°
	right	90°
Hints	Obtuse	90° to 180°
	straight	180°
	reflex	180° to 360°

✏️ *Write the name of the angles.*

1)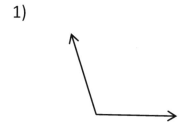

2)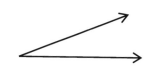

3)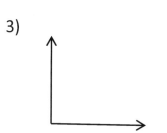

4)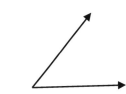

5)

6)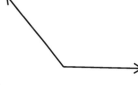

7)

8)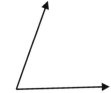

Polygon Names

Helpful Hints	Name	Shape	Name	Shape
	Triangle (or Trigon)	△	Octagon	⬡
	Quadrilateral (or Tetragon)	☐	Nonagon (or Enneagon)	⬠
	Pentagon	⬠	Decagon	⬠
	Hexagon	⬡	Hendecagon (or Undecagon)	⬠
	Heptagon	⬠	Dodecagon	⬠

✏️ Write name of polygons.

1)
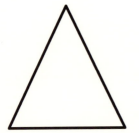

2)

3)
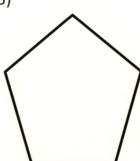

4)

5)
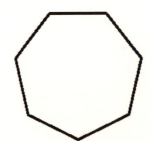

6)
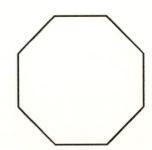

Classify Triangles

Helpful Hints

– Triangles can be classified according to their sides or based on their angles.
According to their sides: Equilateral (has three equal sides), Isosceles (has two equal sides), and Scalene (has three different sides).
According to their angles: Right triangle (has one 90-degree angle), Obtuse triangle (has one angle bigger than 90 degrees), and Acute triangle (has all angles less than 90 degrees).

✍ *Classify the triangles by their sides and angles.*

1)
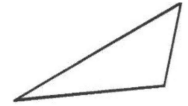

2)
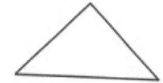

3)
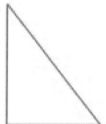

4)
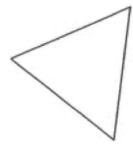

5)
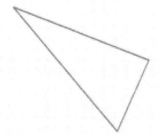

6)
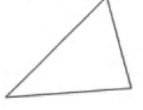

Parallel Sides in Quadrilaterals

Helpful Hints

Quadrilaterals:

Square

Rectangle

Parallelogram

Rhombus

Trapezoid

Kike

✏️ *Write name of quadrilaterals.*

1)

2)

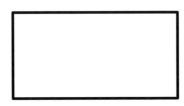

3)

4)

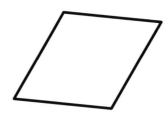

5)

6)

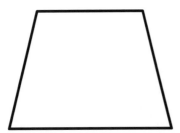
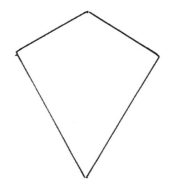

Identify Rectangles

> **Helpful Hints**
> – A rectangle is a quadrilateral with two pairs of congruent parallel sides and four right angles.
>
> **Example:**

✏️ **Solve.**

1) A rectangle has _____ sides and _____ angles.

2) Draw a rectangle that is 6 centimeters long and 3 centimeters wide. What is the perimeter?

3) Draw a rectangle 5 cm long and 2 cm wide.

4) Draw a rectangle whose length is 4 cm and whose width is 2 cm. What is the perimeter of the rectangle?

5) What is the perimeter of the rectangle?

    8
    4

Perimeter: Find the Missing Side Lengths

Helpful Hints

Perimeter of square = 4 × side

Perimeter of rectangles = 2(length + width)

➤ **Find the missing side of each shape.**

1) perimeter = 44

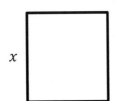

2) perimeter = 28

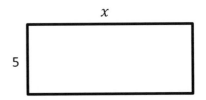

3) perimeter = 30

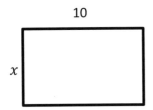

4) perimeter = 16

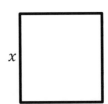

5) perimeter = 60

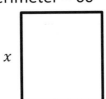

6) perimeter = 22

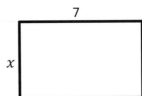

7) perimeter = 30

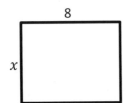

8) perimeter = 36

Perimeter and Area of Squares

Helpful Hints

Perimeter = 4× *side*

Area = (*side*) × (*side*)

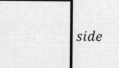 side

✏️ **Find perimeter and area of squares.**

1) A: _____, P: _____

5

2) A: _____, P: _____

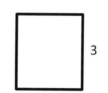
3

3) A: _____, P: _____

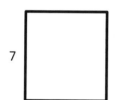
7

4) A: _____, P: _____

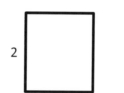
2

5) A: _____, P: _____

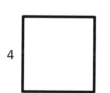
4

6) A: _____, P: _____

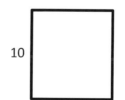
10

7) A: _____, P: _____

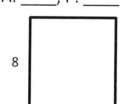
8

8) A: _____, P: _____

12

Perimeter and Area of rectangles

Helpful Hints

P = 2(length + width)

A = length × width

✏️ *Find perimeter and area of rectangles.*

1) A: _____, P: _____

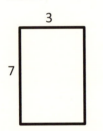 (but for Q1: 10 × 5)

2) A: _____, P: _____

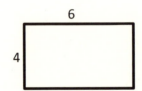

3) A: _____, P: _____

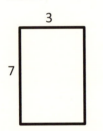

4) A: _____, P: _____

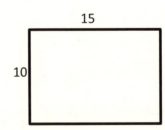

5) A: _____, P: _____

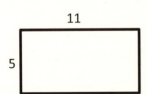

6) A: _____, P: _____

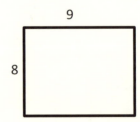

Find the Area or Missing Side Length of a Rectangle

Helpful Hints $A = Width \times Length$

🖊️ Find area or missing side length of rectangles.

1) Area = ?
   14
   5

2) Area = 48, x = ?
   8
   x

3) Area = 40, x = ?
   4
   x

4) Area = ?
   12
   8

5) Area = ?
   22
   15

6) Area = 600, x = ?
   20
   x

7) Area = 384, x = ?
   32
   x

8) Area = 525, x = ?
   x
   21

Area and Perimeter: Word Problems

Helpful Hints

- Area of square = (one side of the square)^2
- Area of Rectangle = length × width
- Perimeter of square = 4 × one side of the square.
- Perimeter of rectangle = 2 × (length + width)

Solve.

1) The area of a rectangle is 72 square meters. The width is 8 meters. What is the length of the rectangle?

2) A square has an area of 36 square feet. What is the perimeter of the square?

3) Ava built a rectangular vegetable garden that is 6 feet long and has an area of 54 square feet. What is the perimeter of Ava's vegetable garden?

4) A square has a perimeter of 64 millimeters. What is the area of the square?

5) The perimeter of David's square backyard is 44 meters. What is the area of David's backyard?

6) The area of a rectangle is 40 square inches. The length is 8 inches. What is the perimeter of the rectangle?

Area of Squares and Rectangles

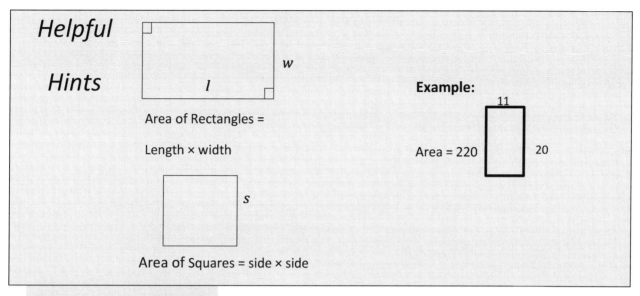

Area of Rectangles = Length × width

Area of Squares = side × side

Example: Area = 220

🖉 *Find the area of each.*

1)

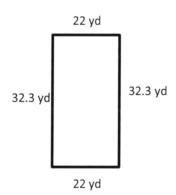

2)

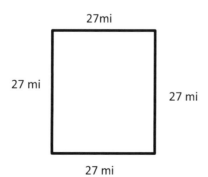

Volume of Cubes and Rectangle Prisms

> **Helpful Hints**
> – Volume is the amount of space inside of a solid figure, like a rectangle prism, cube, or cylinder.
> – Volume of a cube = (one side)^3
> – Volume of a rectangle prism: Length × Width × Height

Find the volume of each of the rectangular prisms.

1)

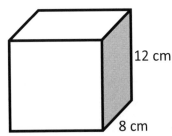

14 cm, 12 cm, 8 cm

2)

22 cm, 15 cm, 5 cm

3)

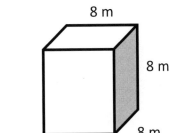

8 m, 8 m, 8 m

4)

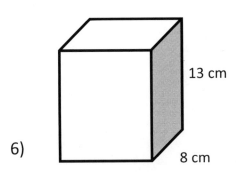

11 cm, 13 cm, 8 cm

5)

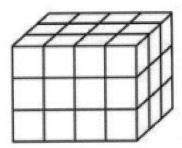

6)

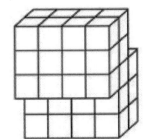

Answers of Worksheets – Chapter 11

Identifying Angles: Acute, Right, Obtuse, and Straight Angles

1) Obtuse
2) Acute
3) Right
4) Acute
5) Straight
6) Obtuse
7) Obtuse
8) Acute

Polygon Names

1) Triangle
2) Quadrilateral
3) Pentagon
4) Hexagon
5) Heptagon
6) Octagon

Classify triangles

1) Scalene, obtuse
2) Isosceles, right
3) Scalene, right
4) Equilateral, acute
5) Scalene, acute
6) Scalene, acute

Parallel Sides in Quadrilaterals

1) Square
2) Rectangle
3) Parallelogram
4) Rhombus
5) Trapezoid
6) Kike

Identify Rectangles

1) 4 - 4
2) 18
3) Use a rule to draw the rectangle
4) 12
5) 24

Perimeter: Find the Missing Side Lengths

1) 11
2) 9
3) 5
4) 4
5) 15
6) 4
7) 7
8) 9

Perimeter and Area of Squares

1) A: 25, P: 20
2) A: 9, P: 12
3) A: 49, P: 28
4) A: 4, P: 8
5) A: 16, P: 16
6) A: 100, P: 40
7) A: 64, P: 32
8) A: 144, P: 48

Perimeter and Area of rectangles

1) A: 50, P: 30
2) A: 24, P: 20
3) A: 21, P: 20
4) A: 150, P: 50
5) A: 55, P: 32
6) A: 72, P: 34

Find the Area or Missing Side Length of a Rectangle

1) 70
2) 6
3) 10
4) 96
5) 330
6) 30
7) 12
8) 25

Area and Perimeter: Word Problems

1) 9
2) 24
3) 30
4) 256
5) 121
6) 26

Area of Squares and Rectangles

1) 710.6 yd^2

2) 729 mi^2

Volume of Cubes and Rectangle Prisms

1) 1344 cm^3

2) 1650 cm^3

3) 512 m^3

4) 1144 cm^3

5) 36

6) 44

Chapter 12: Three-Dimensional Figures

Topics that you'll learn in this chapter:

- ✓ Identify Three–Dimensional Figures
- ✓ Count Vertices, Edges, and Faces
- ✓ Identify Faces of Three–Dimensional Figures

Identify Three–Dimensional Figures

Helpful Hints

– List of figures in this page:
- Square pyramid
- Triangular prism
- Rectangular prism
- Cube
- Triangular pyramid
- Hexagonal prism
- Pentagonal prism

✎ Write the name of each shape.

1)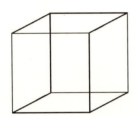

2)

3)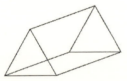

4)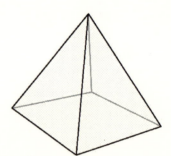

5)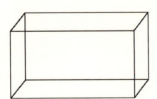

6)

7)

Count Vertices, Edges, and Faces

Helpful Hints
- **Vertex:** the point at which two sides of a polygon meet.
- **Edge:** It's a line segment joining two vertices in a polygon.
- **Face:** It is each flat side of a solid.

	Number of edges	Number of faces	Number of vertices
1)	_____	_____	_____
2)	_____	_____	_____
3)	_____	_____	_____
4)	_____	_____	_____
5)	_____	_____	_____
6)	_____	_____	_____

Identify Faces of Three–Dimensional Figures

> **Helpful Hints**
>
> – A face is a flat surface. All solid figures, with the exception of a sphere, has one or more faces.

✎ **Write the number of faces.**

1)
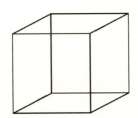

2)

3)
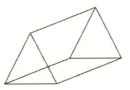

4)

5)
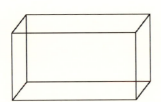

6)

7)

8)

Answers of Worksheets – Chapter 12

Identify Three–Dimensional Figures

1) Cube
2) Triangular pyramid
3) Triangular prism
4) Square pyramid
5) Rectangular prism
6) Pentagonal prism
7) Hexagonal prism

Count Vertices, Edges, and Faces

	Number of edges	Number of faces	Number of vertices
1)	6	4	4
2)	8	5	5
3)	12	6	8
4)	12	6	8

5)    15   7   10

6)    18   8   12

Identify Faces of Three–Dimensional Figures

1) 6
2) 2
3) 5
4) 4
5) 6
6) 7
7) 8
8) 5

Chapter 13: Symmetry and Transformations

Topics that you'll learn in this chapter:

- ✓ Line Segments
- ✓ Identify Lines of Symmetry
- ✓ Count Lines of Symmetry
- ✓ Parallel, Perpendicular and Intersecting Lines

Line Segments

Helpful Hints
- Line segment has a beginning and end points.
- Line doesn't have beginning or end points.
- Ray starts out at a point and continues off to infinity.

✏️ *Write each as a line, ray or line segment.*

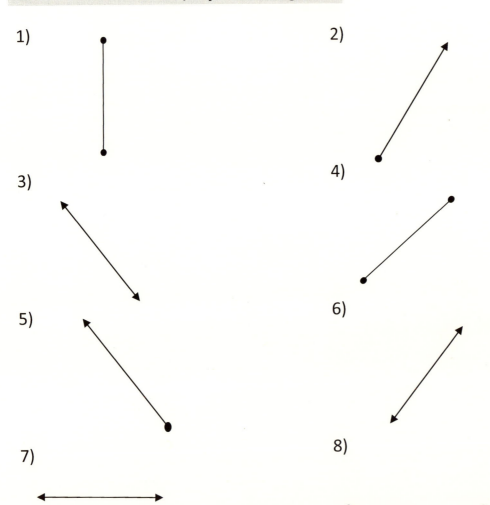

Identify Lines of Symmetry

Helpful Hints — You can find if a shape has a Line of Symmetry by folding it.

✏️ *Tell whether the line on each shape is a line of symmetry.*

1)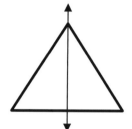

2)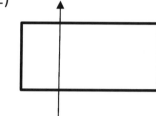

3)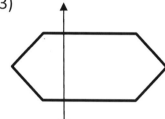

4)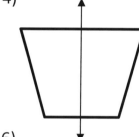

5)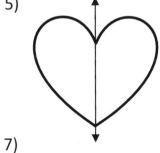

6)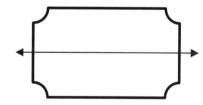

7)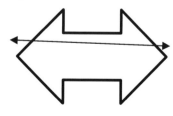

8)

Count Lines of Symmetry

Helpful Hints
- Line of symmetry cuts a shape into two same shapes.
- A shape can have many lines of symmetry.

✎ **Draw lines of symmetry on each shape. Count and write the lines of symmetry you see.**

1)

2)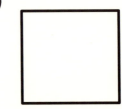

3)

4)

5)

6)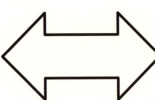

7)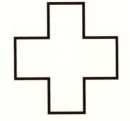

8)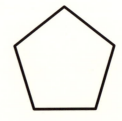

Parallel, Perpendicular and Intersecting Lines

> *Helpful Hints*
>
> – Intersecting lines meet each other at a point.
> – Parallel lines never intersect. They are always equidistant.
> – Perpendicular lines are two lines that intersect to form right angles.

✎ *State whether the given pair of lines are parallel, perpendicular, or intersecting.*

1)

2)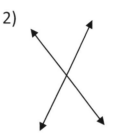

3)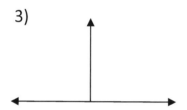

4)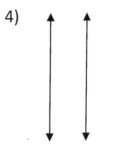

5)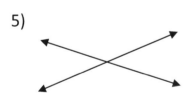

6)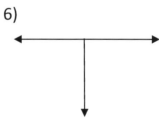

7)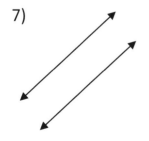

8)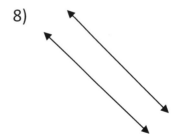

Answers of Worksheets – Chapter 13

Line Segments

1) Line segment
2) Ray
3) Line
4) Line segment
5) Ray
6) Line
7) Line
8) Line segment

Identify lines of symmetry

1) yes
2) no
3) no
4) yes
5) yes
6) yes
7) no
8) yes

Count lines of symmetry

1)

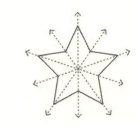

2)

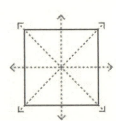

3)

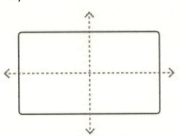

4)

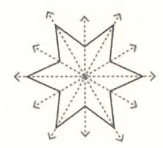

5)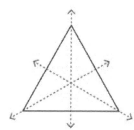

6)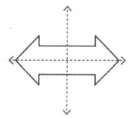

7)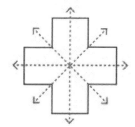

8)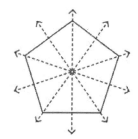

Parallel, Perpendicular and Intersecting Lines

1) Parallel
2) Intersection
3) Perpendicular
4) Parallel
5) Intersection
6) Perpendicular
7) Parallel
8) Parallel

Chapter 14: Fractions

Topics that you'll learn in this chapter:

- ✓ Fractions
- ✓ Add Fractions with Like Denominators
- ✓ Subtract Fractions with Like Denominators
- ✓ Add and Subtract Fractions with Like Denominators
- ✓ Compare Sums and Differences of Fractions with Like Denominators
- ✓ Add 3 or More Fractions with Like Denominators
- ✓ Simplifying Fractions
- ✓ Add Fractions with Unlike Denominators
- ✓ Subtract Fractions with Unlike Denominators
- ✓ Add Fractions with Denominators of 10 and 100
- ✓ Add and Subtract Fractions with Denominators of 10, 100, and 1000

Fractions	
Helpful Hints	- We use fractions for measuring. For example, one third, means one part of three parts of something. - In fractions, we have two numbers. The number in the bottom shows how many parts are in a whole of something. The top number shows how many parts of something have a feature. For example: $\frac{1}{2}$ means half

✎ **What fraction of the squares is shaded?**

1)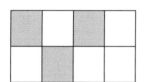

2)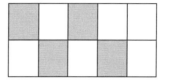

3)

✎ **Which fraction has the least value?**

4) $\frac{1}{3}$ $\frac{2}{7}$ $\frac{8}{21}$ $\frac{4}{42}$

5) $\frac{1}{2}$ $\frac{3}{8}$ $\frac{3}{4}$ $\frac{9}{16}$

Add Fractions with Like Denominators

> **Helpful Hints** — Adding with the same denominator:
> $$\frac{1}{6}+\frac{2}{6}=\frac{1+2}{6}=\frac{3}{6}$$
> Example:
> $$\frac{2}{5}+\frac{1}{5}=\frac{2+1}{5}=\frac{3}{5}$$

✎ Add fractions.

1) $\dfrac{2}{3}+\dfrac{1}{3}$

2) $\dfrac{3}{5}+\dfrac{2}{5}$

3) $\dfrac{5}{8}+\dfrac{4}{8}$

4) $\dfrac{3}{4}+\dfrac{3}{4}$

5) $\dfrac{4}{10}+\dfrac{3}{10}$

6) $\dfrac{3}{7}+\dfrac{2}{7}$

7) $\dfrac{4}{5}+\dfrac{4}{5}$

8) $\dfrac{5}{14}+\dfrac{7}{14}$

9) $\dfrac{5}{18}+\dfrac{11}{18}$

10) $\dfrac{3}{12}+\dfrac{5}{12}$

11) $\dfrac{5}{13}+\dfrac{5}{13}$

12) $\dfrac{8}{25}+\dfrac{12}{25}$

13) $\dfrac{9}{15}+\dfrac{6}{15}$

14) $\dfrac{4}{20}+\dfrac{5}{20}$

15) $\dfrac{9}{17}+\dfrac{3}{17}$

16) $\dfrac{18}{32}+\dfrac{15}{32}$

17) $\dfrac{12}{28}+\dfrac{10}{28}$

18) $\dfrac{4}{20}+\dfrac{8}{20}$

19) $\dfrac{24}{45}+\dfrac{11}{45}$

20) $\dfrac{8}{36}+\dfrac{18}{36}$

21) $\dfrac{19}{30}+\dfrac{12}{30}$

Subtract Fractions with Like Denominators

Helpful Hints

- Subtracting with the same denominator:

$$\frac{5}{6} - \frac{1}{6} = \frac{5-1}{6} = \frac{4}{6}$$

Example:

$$\frac{4}{7} - \frac{2}{7} = \frac{2}{7}$$

✎ *Subtract fractions.*

1) $\dfrac{4}{5} - \dfrac{2}{5}$

2) $\dfrac{2}{3} - \dfrac{1}{3}$

3) $\dfrac{7}{9} - \dfrac{4}{9}$

4) $\dfrac{5}{6} - \dfrac{3}{6}$

5) $\dfrac{4}{10} - \dfrac{3}{10}$

6) $\dfrac{5}{7} - \dfrac{3}{7}$

7) $\dfrac{7}{8} - \dfrac{5}{8}$

8) $\dfrac{11}{13} - \dfrac{9}{13}$

9) $\dfrac{8}{10} - \dfrac{5}{10}$

10) $\dfrac{8}{12} - \dfrac{7}{12}$

11) $\dfrac{18}{21} - \dfrac{12}{21}$

12) $\dfrac{15}{19} - \dfrac{9}{19}$

13) $\dfrac{9}{25} - \dfrac{6}{25}$

14) $\dfrac{25}{32} - \dfrac{17}{32}$

15) $\dfrac{22}{27} - \dfrac{9}{27}$

16) $\dfrac{27}{30} - \dfrac{15}{30}$

17) $\dfrac{31}{33} - \dfrac{26}{33}$

18) $\dfrac{18}{28} - \dfrac{8}{28}$

19) $\dfrac{35}{40} - \dfrac{15}{40}$

20) $\dfrac{29}{35} - \dfrac{19}{35}$

21) $\dfrac{21}{36} - \dfrac{11}{36}$

Add and Subtract Fractions with Like Denominators

Helpful Hints

- Adding and Subtracting with the same denominator:

$$\frac{a}{b} + \frac{c}{b} = \frac{a+c}{b}$$

$$\frac{a}{b} - \frac{c}{b} = \frac{a-c}{b}$$

Example:

$$\frac{3}{12} - \frac{1}{12} = \frac{2}{12}$$

$$\frac{7}{9} - \frac{3}{9} = \frac{4}{9}$$

✏ Add fractions.

1) $\frac{1}{3} + \frac{2}{3}$

2) $\frac{3}{6} + \frac{2}{6}$

3) $\frac{5}{8} + \frac{2}{8}$

4) $\frac{3}{9} + \frac{5}{9}$

5) $\frac{4}{10} + \frac{1}{10}$

6) $\frac{3}{7} + \frac{2}{7}$

7) $\frac{3}{5} + \frac{2}{5}$

8) $\frac{1}{12} + \frac{1}{12}$

9) $\frac{16}{25} + \frac{5}{25}$

✏ Subtract fractions.

10) $\frac{4}{5} - \frac{2}{5}$

11) $\frac{5}{7} - \frac{3}{7}$

12) $\frac{3}{4} - \frac{2}{4}$

13) $\frac{8}{9} - \frac{3}{9}$

14) $\frac{6}{14} - \frac{3}{14}$

15) $\frac{4}{15} - \frac{1}{15}$

16) $\frac{15}{16} - \frac{13}{16}$

17) $\frac{25}{50} - \frac{20}{50}$

18) $\frac{10}{21} - \frac{7}{21}$

Compare Sums and Differences of Fractions with Like Denominators

Helpful Hints

- When fractions have same denominators (the bottom number), the one with bigger numerator (the top number) is greater.

Example:

$\dfrac{3}{7} > \dfrac{2}{7}$

✎ Evaluate and compare. Write < or > or =.

1) $\dfrac{1}{4} + \dfrac{2}{4}$ — $\dfrac{1}{4}$

2) $\dfrac{3}{5} + \dfrac{2}{5}$ — $\dfrac{4}{5}$

3) $\dfrac{5}{7} - \dfrac{3}{7}$ — $\dfrac{6}{7}$

4) $\dfrac{9}{10} + \dfrac{7}{10}$ — $\dfrac{5}{10}$

5) $\dfrac{5}{9} - \dfrac{3}{9}$ — $\dfrac{7}{9}$

6) $\dfrac{10}{12} - \dfrac{5}{12}$ — $\dfrac{3}{12}$

7) $\dfrac{3}{8} + \dfrac{1}{8}$ — $\dfrac{1}{8}$

8) $\dfrac{10}{15} + \dfrac{4}{15}$ — $\dfrac{9}{15}$

9) $\dfrac{15}{18} - \dfrac{3}{18}$ — $\dfrac{17}{18}$

10) $\dfrac{17}{21} + \dfrac{4}{21}$ — $\dfrac{18}{21}$

11) $\dfrac{14}{16} - \dfrac{4}{16}$ — $\dfrac{12}{16}$

12) $\dfrac{27}{32} - \dfrac{11}{32}$ — $\dfrac{20}{32}$

13) $\dfrac{25}{30} + \dfrac{5}{30}$ — $\dfrac{15}{30}$

14) $\dfrac{25}{27} - \dfrac{3}{27}$ — $\dfrac{9}{27}$

15) $\dfrac{42}{45} - \dfrac{15}{45}$ — $\dfrac{30}{45}$

16) $\dfrac{32}{36} + \dfrac{15}{36}$ — $\dfrac{18}{36}$

Add 3 or More Fractions with Like Denominators

Helpful Hints
- For fractions with same denominators, you only need to add the numerator (the tope number).
- The denominator (the bottom number) of the answer will be the same.

Example:
$$\frac{3}{11} + \frac{2}{11} + \frac{5}{11} = \frac{3+2+5}{11} = \frac{10}{11}$$

✎ Add fractions.

1) $\frac{4}{7} + \frac{2}{7} + \frac{1}{7}$

2) $\frac{1}{5} + \frac{3}{5} + \frac{1}{5}$

3) $\frac{3}{9} + \frac{3}{9} + \frac{1}{9}$

4) $\frac{1}{4} + \frac{1}{4} + \frac{1}{4}$

5) $\frac{7}{15} + \frac{3}{15} + \frac{4}{15}$

6) $\frac{3}{12} + \frac{2}{12} + \frac{3}{12}$

7) $\frac{4}{10} + \frac{2}{10} + \frac{1}{10}$

8) $\frac{5}{18} + \frac{5}{18} + \frac{3}{18}$

9) $\frac{5}{21} + \frac{11}{21} + \frac{3}{21}$

10) $\frac{2}{16} + \frac{5}{16} + \frac{8}{16}$

11) $\frac{4}{25} + \frac{4}{25} + \frac{4}{25}$

12) $\frac{12}{30} + \frac{7}{30} + \frac{5}{30}$

13) $\frac{9}{27} + \frac{6}{27} + \frac{6}{27}$

14) $\frac{3}{42} + \frac{5}{42} + \frac{6}{42}$

Simplifying Fractions

Helpful Hints
– Evenly divide both the top and bottom of the fraction by 2, 3, 5, 7, ... etc.
– Continue until you can't go any further.

Example:
$$\frac{4}{12} = \frac{2}{6} = \frac{1}{3}$$

✎ Simplify the fractions.

1) $\frac{22}{36}$

2) $\frac{8}{10}$

3) $\frac{12}{18}$

4) $\frac{6}{8}$

5) $\frac{13}{39}$

6) $\frac{5}{20}$

7) $\frac{16}{36}$

8) $\frac{18}{36}$

9) $\frac{20}{50}$

10) $\frac{6}{54}$

11) $\frac{45}{81}$

12) $\frac{21}{28}$

13) $\frac{35}{56}$

14) $\frac{52}{64}$

15) $\frac{13}{65}$

16) $\frac{44}{77}$

17) $\frac{21}{42}$

18) $\frac{15}{36}$

19) $\frac{9}{24}$

20) $\frac{20}{80}$

21) $\frac{25}{45}$

Add Fractions with Unlike Denominators

Helpful Hints

Adding fraction with the different denominator:

$$\frac{a}{b} + \frac{c}{d} = \frac{ad + cb}{bd}$$

Example:

$$\frac{3}{4} + \frac{2}{3} = \frac{9+8}{12} = \frac{17}{12}$$

✎ *Add fractions.*

1) $\frac{2}{3} + \frac{1}{2}$

2) $\frac{3}{5} + \frac{1}{6}$

3) $\frac{5}{6} + \frac{1}{2}$

4) $\frac{3}{4} + \frac{5}{9}$

5) $\frac{2}{5} + \frac{1}{6}$

6) $\frac{3}{7} + \frac{1}{3}$

7) $\frac{3}{4} + \frac{2}{5}$

8) $\frac{2}{3} + \frac{1}{5}$

9) $\frac{16}{25} + \frac{3}{20}$

10) $\frac{2}{7} + \frac{1}{2}$

11) $\frac{3}{11} + \frac{2}{5}$

12) $\frac{1}{3} + \frac{1}{15}$

Subtract Fractions with Unlike Denominators

Helpful Hints

Subtracting fractions with the different denominators:

$$\frac{a}{b} - \frac{c}{d} = \frac{ad - cb}{bd}$$

Example:

$$\frac{5}{12} - \frac{2}{6} = \frac{5-4}{12} = \frac{1}{12}$$

✏ Subtract fractions.

1) $\dfrac{4}{5} - \dfrac{1}{3}$

2) $\dfrac{3}{5} - \dfrac{3}{7}$

3) $\dfrac{1}{2} - \dfrac{1}{3}$

4) $\dfrac{8}{9} - \dfrac{3}{5}$

5) $\dfrac{3}{7} - \dfrac{3}{14}$

6) $\dfrac{4}{15} - \dfrac{1}{10}$

7) $\dfrac{13}{18} - \dfrac{2}{3}$

8) $\dfrac{5}{8} - \dfrac{2}{5}$

9) $\dfrac{1}{2} - \dfrac{1}{9}$

10) $\dfrac{13}{25} - \dfrac{1}{5}$

11) $\dfrac{1}{3} - \dfrac{1}{27}$

12) $\dfrac{11}{20} - \dfrac{2}{7}$

Add Fractions with Denominators of 10 and 100

Helpful Hints

Adding fractions with the different denominators:

$$\frac{a}{b} + \frac{c}{d} = \frac{ad + cb}{bd}$$

Example:

$$\frac{7}{10} + \frac{20}{100} = \frac{70 + 20}{100}$$
$$= \frac{90}{100}$$

✎ **Add fractions.**

1) $\frac{5}{10} + \frac{20}{100}$

2) $\frac{2}{10} + \frac{35}{100}$

3) $\frac{25}{100} + \frac{6}{10}$

4) $\frac{73}{100} + \frac{1}{10}$

5) $\frac{68}{100} + \frac{2}{10}$

6) $\frac{4}{10} + \frac{40}{100}$

7) $\frac{80}{100} + \frac{1}{10}$

8) $\frac{50}{100} + \frac{3}{10}$

9) $\frac{59}{100} + \frac{3}{10}$

10) $\frac{7}{10} + \frac{12}{100}$

11) $\frac{9}{10} + \frac{10}{100}$

12) $\frac{40}{100} + \frac{3}{10}$

13) $\frac{36}{100} + \frac{4}{10}$

14) $\frac{27}{100} + \frac{6}{10}$

15) $\frac{55}{100} + \frac{3}{10}$

16) $\frac{1}{10} + \frac{85}{100}$

17) $\frac{17}{100} + \frac{6}{10}$

18) $\frac{26}{100} + \frac{7}{10}$

Add and Subtract Fractions with Denominators of 10, 100, and 1000

Helpful Hints

Adding and subtracting fractions with the different denominators:

$$\frac{a}{b} + \frac{c}{d} = \frac{ad + cb}{bd}$$

$$\frac{a}{b} - \frac{c}{d} = \frac{ad - cb}{bd}$$

Example:

$$\frac{5}{100} - \frac{30}{1000} = \frac{50 - 30}{1000} = \frac{20}{1000}$$

✎ Evaluate fractions.

1) $\dfrac{8}{10} - \dfrac{30}{100}$

2) $\dfrac{6}{10} + \dfrac{27}{100}$

3) $\dfrac{25}{100} + \dfrac{450}{1000}$

4) $\dfrac{73}{100} - \dfrac{320}{1000}$

5) $\dfrac{25}{100} + \dfrac{670}{1000}$

6) $\dfrac{4}{10} + \dfrac{780}{1000}$

7) $\dfrac{80}{100} - \dfrac{560}{1000}$

8) $\dfrac{78}{100} - \dfrac{6}{10}$

9) $\dfrac{820}{1000} + \dfrac{5}{10}$

10) $\dfrac{67}{100} + \dfrac{240}{1000}$

11) $\dfrac{7}{10} - \dfrac{12}{100}$

12) $\dfrac{75}{100} - \dfrac{5}{10}$

13) $\dfrac{70}{100} - \dfrac{3}{10}$

14) $\dfrac{850}{1000} - \dfrac{5}{100}$

15) $\dfrac{300}{1000} + \dfrac{12}{100}$

16) $\dfrac{780}{1000} - \dfrac{6}{10}$

17) $\dfrac{80}{100} - \dfrac{6}{10}$

18) $\dfrac{50}{100} - \dfrac{210}{1000}$

Answers of Worksheets – Chapter 14

Fraction

1) $\frac{3}{8}$
2) $\frac{4}{10}$
3) $\frac{6}{20}$
4) $\frac{4}{42}$
5) $\frac{3}{8}$

Add Fractions with Like Denominators

1) 1
2) 1
3) $\frac{9}{8}$
4) $\frac{6}{4}$
5) $\frac{7}{10}$
6) $\frac{5}{7}$
7) $\frac{8}{5}$
8) $\frac{12}{14}$
9) $\frac{16}{18}$
10) $\frac{8}{12}$
11) $\frac{10}{13}$
12) $\frac{20}{25}$
13) 1
14) $\frac{9}{20}$
15) $\frac{12}{17}$
16) $\frac{33}{32}$
17) $\frac{22}{28}$
18) $\frac{12}{20}$
19) $\frac{35}{45}$
20) $\frac{26}{36}$
21) $\frac{31}{30}$

Subtract Fractions with Like Denominators

1) $\frac{2}{5}$
2) $\frac{1}{3}$
3) $\frac{3}{9}$
4) $\frac{2}{6}$
5) $\frac{1}{10}$
6) $\frac{2}{7}$
7) $\frac{2}{8}$
8) $\frac{2}{13}$
9) $\frac{3}{10}$
10) $\frac{1}{12}$
11) $\frac{6}{21}$
12) $\frac{6}{19}$

13) $\frac{3}{25}$

14) $\frac{1}{4}$

15) $\frac{13}{27}$

16) $\frac{12}{30}$

17) $\frac{5}{33}$

18) $\frac{10}{28}$

19) $\frac{20}{40}$

20) $\frac{2}{7}$

21) $\frac{10}{36}$

Add and Subtract Fractions with Like Denominators

1) 1

2) $\frac{5}{6}$

3) $\frac{7}{8}$

4) $\frac{8}{9}$

5) $\frac{5}{10}$

6) $\frac{5}{7}$

7) 1

8) $\frac{2}{12}$

9) $\frac{21}{25}$

10) $\frac{2}{5}$

11) $\frac{2}{7}$

12) $\frac{1}{4}$

13) $\frac{5}{9}$

14) $\frac{3}{14}$

15) $\frac{3}{15}$

16) $\frac{2}{16}$

17) $\frac{5}{50}$

18) $\frac{3}{21}$

Compare Sums and Differences of Fractions with Like Denominators

1) $\frac{3}{4} > \frac{1}{4}$

2) $1 > \frac{4}{5}$

3) $\frac{2}{7} < \frac{6}{7}$

4) $\frac{16}{10} > \frac{5}{10}$

5) $\frac{2}{9} < \frac{7}{9}$

6) $\frac{5}{12} > \frac{3}{12}$

7) $\frac{4}{8} > \frac{1}{8}$

8) $\frac{14}{15} > \frac{9}{15}$

9) $\frac{12}{18} < \frac{17}{18}$

10) $1 > \frac{18}{21}$

11) $\frac{10}{16} < \frac{12}{16}$

12) $\frac{16}{32} < \frac{20}{32}$

13) $1 > \frac{15}{30}$

14) $\frac{22}{27} > \frac{9}{27}$

15) $\frac{27}{45} < \frac{30}{45}$

16) $\dfrac{47}{36} > \dfrac{18}{36}$

Add 3 or More Fractions with Like Denominators

1) 1

2) 1

3) $\dfrac{7}{9}$

4) $\dfrac{3}{4}$

5) $\dfrac{14}{15}$

6) $\dfrac{8}{12}$

7) $\dfrac{7}{10}$

8) $\dfrac{13}{18}$

9) $\dfrac{19}{21}$

10) $\dfrac{15}{16}$

11) $\dfrac{12}{25}$

12) $\dfrac{24}{30}$

13) $\dfrac{21}{27}$

14) $\dfrac{14}{42}$

Simplifying Fractions

1) $\dfrac{11}{18}$

2) $\dfrac{4}{5}$

3) $\dfrac{2}{3}$

4) $\dfrac{3}{4}$

5) $\dfrac{1}{3}$

6) $\dfrac{1}{4}$

7) $\dfrac{4}{9}$

8) $\dfrac{1}{2}$

9) $\dfrac{2}{5}$

10) $\dfrac{1}{9}$

11) $\dfrac{5}{9}$

12) $\dfrac{3}{4}$

13) $\dfrac{5}{8}$

14) $\dfrac{13}{16}$

15) $\dfrac{1}{5}$

16) $\dfrac{4}{7}$

17) $\dfrac{1}{2}$

18) $\dfrac{5}{12}$

19) $\frac{3}{8}$ 20) $\frac{1}{4}$ 21) $\frac{5}{9}$

Add fractions with unlike denominators

1) $\frac{7}{6}$ 5) $\frac{17}{30}$ 9) $\frac{79}{100}$

2) $\frac{23}{30}$ 6) $\frac{16}{21}$ 10) $\frac{11}{14}$

3) $\frac{4}{3}$ 7) $\frac{23}{20}$ 11) $\frac{37}{55}$

4) $\frac{47}{36}$ 8) $\frac{13}{15}$ 12) $\frac{2}{5}$

Subtract fractions with unlike denominators

1) $\frac{7}{15}$ 5) $\frac{3}{14}$ 9) $\frac{7}{18}$

2) $\frac{6}{35}$ 6) $\frac{1}{6}$ 10) $\frac{8}{25}$

3) $\frac{1}{6}$ 7) $\frac{1}{18}$ 11) $\frac{8}{27}$

4) $\frac{13}{45}$ 8) $\frac{9}{40}$ 12) $\frac{37}{140}$

Add fractions with denominators of 10 and 100

1) $\frac{7}{10}$ 4) $\frac{83}{100}$ 7) $\frac{9}{10}$

2) $\frac{11}{20}$ 5) $\frac{22}{25}$ 8) $\frac{4}{5}$

3) $\frac{17}{20}$ 6) $\frac{4}{5}$ 9) $\frac{89}{100}$

10) $\dfrac{41}{50}$

11) 1

12) $\dfrac{7}{10}$

13) $\dfrac{19}{25}$

14) $\dfrac{87}{100}$

15) $\dfrac{17}{20}$

16) $\dfrac{19}{20}$

17) $\dfrac{77}{100}$

18) $\dfrac{24}{25}$

Add and subtract fractions with denominators of 10, 100, and 1000

1) $\dfrac{50}{100}$

2) $\dfrac{87}{100}$

3) $\dfrac{7}{10}$

4) $\dfrac{41}{100}$

5) $\dfrac{23}{25}$

6) $\dfrac{59}{50}$

7) $\dfrac{6}{25}$

8) $\dfrac{9}{50}$

9) $\dfrac{33}{25}$

10) $\dfrac{91}{100}$

11) $\dfrac{29}{50}$

12) $\dfrac{1}{4}$

13) $\dfrac{2}{5}$

14) $\dfrac{4}{5}$

15) $\dfrac{21}{50}$

16) $\dfrac{9}{50}$

17) $\dfrac{1}{5}$

18) $\dfrac{29}{100}$

Chapter 15: Mixed Numbers

Topics that you'll learn in this chapter:

- ✓ Fractions to Mixed Numbers
- ✓ Mixed Numbers to Fractions
- ✓ Add and Subtract Mixed Numbers

Fractions to Mixed Numbers

> **Helpful Hints**
> - Divide the numerator by the denominator.
> - Write down the whole number of the answer.
> - Then write down any remainder above the denominator.
>
> **Example:**
> $\frac{7}{6} = 1\frac{1}{6}$

✍ **Convert fractions to mixed numbers.**

1) $\frac{9}{4}$

2) $\frac{37}{5}$

3) $\frac{21}{6}$

4) $\frac{41}{10}$

5) $\frac{11}{2}$

6) $\frac{56}{10}$

7) $\frac{20}{12}$

8) $\frac{9}{5}$

9) $\frac{19}{5}$

10) $\frac{27}{10}$

11) $\frac{10}{6}$

12) $\frac{17}{8}$

13) $\frac{7}{2}$

14) $\frac{39}{4}$

15) $\frac{72}{10}$

16) $\frac{13}{3}$

17) $\frac{45}{8}$

18) $\frac{27}{5}$

Mixed Numbers to Fractions

Helpful Hints
- Multiply the whole number part by the fraction's denominator.
- Add the result to the numerator.
- Write that result on top of the denominator.

Example:

$$2\frac{3}{4} = \frac{11}{6}$$

✎ **Convert to fraction.**

1) $1\frac{2}{6}$

2) $2\frac{2}{3}$

3) $5\frac{1}{3}$

4) $6\frac{4}{5}$

5) $2\frac{3}{4}$

6) $2\frac{5}{7}$

7) $3\frac{5}{9}$

8) $2\frac{9}{10}$

9) $7\frac{5}{6}$

10) $6\frac{11}{12}$

11) $8\frac{9}{20}$

12) $8\frac{2}{5}$

13) $5\frac{4}{5}$

14) $9\frac{1}{6}$

15) $3\frac{3}{4}$

16) $10\frac{2}{3}$

17) $12\frac{3}{4}$

18) $14\frac{6}{7}$

Add and Subtract Mixed Numbers

Helpful Hints
- Add whole numbers.
- Add numerators and write the result on top of the common denominator.
- If the answer is an improper fraction (the denominator is smaller than numerator), reduce the fraction into a mixed number.
- Simplify if necessary.

Example:

✎ *Add mixed numbers.*

1) $5\frac{2}{9} + 8\frac{1}{2}$

2) $4\frac{1}{2} + 6\frac{4}{5}$

3) $6\frac{1}{3} + 7\frac{1}{4}$

4) $5\frac{1}{2} + 8\frac{1}{3}$

5) $5\frac{1}{3} - 1\frac{2}{3}$

6) $7\frac{3}{20} - 1\frac{3}{5}$

7) $7\frac{5}{9} - 2\frac{7}{9}$

8) $4\frac{4}{5} - 2\frac{9}{10}$

9) $5\frac{23}{25} - 1\frac{12}{25}$

10) $6\frac{2}{7} + 4\frac{1}{2}$

11) $3\frac{3}{8} + 2\frac{1}{8}$

12) $6\frac{2}{7} + 2\frac{1}{5}$

Answers of Worksheets – Chapter 15

Fractions to Mixed Numbers

1) $2\frac{1}{4}$
2) $7\frac{2}{5}$
3) $3\frac{1}{2}$
4) $4\frac{1}{10}$
5) $5\frac{1}{2}$
6) $5\frac{3}{5}$
7) $1\frac{2}{3}$
8) $1\frac{4}{5}$
9) $3\frac{4}{5}$
10) $2\frac{7}{10}$
11) $1\frac{2}{3}$
12) $2\frac{1}{8}$
13) $3\frac{1}{2}$
14) $9\frac{3}{4}$
15) $7\frac{1}{5}$
16) $4\frac{1}{3}$
17) $5\frac{5}{8}$
18) $5\frac{2}{5}$

Mixed Numbers to Fractions

1) $\frac{4}{3}$
2) $\frac{8}{3}$
3) $\frac{16}{3}$
4) $\frac{34}{5}$
5) $\frac{11}{4}$
6) $\frac{19}{7}$
7) $\frac{32}{9}$
8) $\frac{29}{10}$
9) $\frac{47}{6}$
10) $\frac{83}{12}$
11) $\frac{169}{20}$
12) $\frac{42}{5}$
13) $\frac{29}{5}$
14) $\frac{55}{6}$
15) $\frac{15}{4}$

16) $\dfrac{32}{3}$ 17) $\dfrac{51}{4}$ 18) $\dfrac{104}{7}$

Add and Subtract Mixed Numbers with Like Denominators

1) $13\dfrac{13}{18}$ 5) $3\dfrac{2}{3}$ 9) $4\dfrac{11}{25}$

2) $11\dfrac{3}{10}$ 6) $5\dfrac{11}{20}$ 10) $10\dfrac{11}{14}$

3) $13\dfrac{7}{12}$ 7) $4\dfrac{7}{9}$ 11) $5\dfrac{1}{2}$

4) $13\dfrac{5}{6}$ 8) $1\dfrac{9}{10}$ 12) $8\dfrac{17}{35}$

Chapter 16: Decimal

Topics that you'll learn in this chapter:

- ✓ Decimal Place Value
- ✓ Ordering and Comparing Decimals
- ✓ Decimal Addition
- ✓ Decimal Subtraction

Decimal Place Value

Helpful Hints

- You can round decimals to a number of decimal places. This makes calculation easier when the exact answer is not too important.
- Remember, you'll need to find the place values.
- Let's review some place values.

$$12.3456$$

1: tens
2: ones
3: tenths
4: hundredths
5: thousandths
6: ten thousandths

✎ *What place is the selected digit?*

1) 1,12<u>2</u>.25

2) 2,321.3<u>2</u>

3) 4,258.9<u>1</u>

4) 6,3<u>7</u>2.67

5) 7,131.<u>9</u>8

6) <u>5</u>,442.73

7) 1,841.8<u>9</u>

8) 5,995.<u>76</u>

9) 8,<u>9</u>82.55

10) 1,24<u>9</u>.21

✎ *What is the value of the selected digit?*

11) 3,122.3<u>1</u>

12) 1,3<u>1</u>8.66

13) 6,352.<u>2</u>5

14) 3,<u>7</u>39.16

15) 4,9<u>3</u>6.78

16) 7,6<u>2</u>5.86

17) 9,313.4<u>5</u>

18) <u>2</u>,168.82

19) 8,<u>4</u>51.76

20) 2,153.<u>23</u>

Ordering and Comparing Decimals

Helpful Hints

- **Decimals:** is a fraction written in a special form. For example, instead of writing $\frac{1}{2}$ you can write 0.5.
- **For comparing:**
  Equal to =
  Less than <
  Greater than >
  Greater than or equal ≥
  Less than or equal ≤

Example:

2.67 > 0.267

✏ Use > = <.

1) 0.23 ___ 0.34
2) 0.31 ___ 0.37
3) 0.55 ___ 0.47
4) 0.57 ___ 0.59
5) 0.56 ___ 0.67
6) 0.7 ___ 0.67

7) 0.96 ___ 8.55
8) 0.59 ___ 0.88
9) 0.5 ___ 0.25
10) 0.6 ___ 0.3
11) 0.75 ___ 0.6
12) 0.8 ___ 0.80

13) 0.59 ___ 0.6
14) 0.57 ___ 0.75
15) 0.9 ___ 0.11
16) 0.40 ___ 0.4

✏ Order each set of integers from least to greatest.

17) 0.4, 0.54, 0.23, 0.87, 0.36   ___, ___, ___, ___, ___, ___

18) 1.2, 2.4, 1.97, 3.65, 1.80   ___, ___, ___, ___, ___, ___

19) 2.3, 1.2, 1.9, 0.67, 0.34   ___, ___, ___, ___, ___, ___

20) 1.7, 1.2, 3.2, 4.2, 1.34, 3.55   ___, ___, ___, ___, ___, ___

Decimal Addition

Helpful Hints	1– Line up the numbers. 2– Add zeros to have same number of digits for both numbers. 3– Add using column addition or subtraction.	Example: 12.22 $\underline{+\ 10.34}$ 22.56

✎ Add.

1) 8.12 + 5.24 =

2) 1.5 + 1.3 =

3) 7.2 + 1.34 =

4) 3.4 + 1.75 =

5) 2.55 + 5.25 =

6) 5.78 + 4.30 =

7) 12.45 + 14.25 =

8) 13.67 + 11.31 =

9) 16.25 + 12.34 =

10) 10.25 + 12.55 =

11) 21.25 + 20.90 =

12) 16.25 + 12.88 =

13) 18.44 + 12.65 =

14) 32.2 + 20.45 =

15) 15.76 + 15.98 =

16) 25.5 + 23.9 =

17) 30.95 + 21.40 =

18) 23.6 + 21.6 =

Decimal Subtraction

Helpful Hints	1– Line up the numbers. 2– Add zeros to have same number of digits for both numbers. 3– Subtract using column addition or subtraction.	Example: $\quad\;\;16.18$ $-\;13.45$ $\overline{\quad\;\;\;2.73}$

✏️ *Subtract.*

1) 6.2 − 3.54 =

2) 5.77 − 4.32 =

3) 8.66 − 6.55 =

4) 7.34 − 3.22 =

5) 4.5 − 2.1 =

6) 3.78 − 2.55 =

7) 5.98 − 4.44 =

8) 4.23 − 3.9 =

9) 16.5 − 13.12 =

10) 18.67 − 11.35 =

11) 12.98 − 10.45 =

12) 14.2 − 12.4 =

13) 20.14 − 18.2 =

14) 25.6 − 24.2 =

15) 21.88 − 20.12 =

16) 27.55 − 23.4 =

17) 31.34 − 27.21 =

18) 23.34 − 21.5 =

Answers of Worksheets – Chapter 16

Decimal Place Value

1) one
2) hundredths
3) hundredths
4) tenths
5) tenths
6) thousands
7) hundredths
8) tenths
9) hundredths
10) ones
11) 0.01
12) 10
13) 0.2
14) 700
15) 30
16) 5
17) 0.05
18) 2,000
19) 400
20) 0.2

Order and Comparing Decimals

1) <
2) <
3) >
4) <
5) <
6) >
7) <
8) <
9) >
10) >
11) >
12) =
13) <
14) <
15) >
16) =

17) 0.23, 0.36, 0.4, 0.54, 0.87
18) 1.2, 1.80, 1.97, 2.4, 3.65
19) 0.34, 0.67, 1.2, 1.9, 2.3
20) 1.2, 1.34, 1.7, 3.2, 3.55, 4.2

Decimal Addition

1) 13.36
2) 2.8
3) 8.54
4) 5.15
5) 7.80
6) 10.08
7) 26.7
8) 24.98
9) 28.59
10) 22.80
11) 42.15
12) 29.13
13) 31.09
14) 52.65
15) 31.74
16) 49.4
17) 52.35
18) 45.2

Decimal Subtraction

1) 2.66
2) 1.45
3) 2.11
4) 4.12
5) 2.4
6) 1.23
7) 1.54
8) 0.33
9) 3.38
10) 7.32
11) 2.53
12) 1.8
13) 1.94
14) 1.4
15) 1.76
16) 4.15
17) 4.13
18) 1.84

SSAT Lower Level Quantitative Practice Tests

The SSAT, or Secondary School Admissions Test, is a standardized test to help determine admission to private elementary, middle and high schools.

There are currently three Levels of the SSAT:

- ✓ Lower Level (for students in 3rd and 4th grade)
- ✓ Middle Level (for students in 5th-7th grade)
- ✓ Upper Level (for students in 8th-11th grade)

There are four sections on the SSAT Lower Level Test:

- ✓ Quantitative section: 30 questions, 30 minutes.
- ✓ Verbal section: 30 questions, 20 minutes.
- ✓ Reading section: 7 short passages, 28 questions, 30 minutes.
- ✓ Writing sample: 15 minutes to write a short passage

In this book, we have reviewed mathematics topics being tested on the quantitative (math) section of the SSAT Middle Level. In this section, there are two complete SSAT Lower Level Quantitative Tests. Let your student take these tests to see what score they will be able to receive on a real SSAT Lower Level test.

Good luck!

Time to Test

Time to refine your skill with a practice examination

Take two practice SSAT Lower Level Mathematics Tests to simulate the test day experience. After you've finished, score your test using the answer key.

Before You Start

- You'll need a pencil and a timer to take the test.
- After you've finished the test, review the answer key to see where you went wrong.
- You will receive 1 point for every correct answer. You won't receive any point for wrong or skipped answers.

Calculators are NOT permitted for the SSAT Lower Level Test

Good Luck!

SSAT Lower Level Mathematics Practice Tests Answer Sheet

SSAT Lower Level Practice Test 1

#	A B C D E	#	A B C D E	#	A B C D E
1	Ⓐ Ⓑ Ⓒ Ⓓ Ⓔ	11	Ⓐ Ⓑ Ⓒ Ⓓ Ⓔ	21	Ⓐ Ⓑ Ⓒ Ⓓ Ⓔ
2	Ⓐ Ⓑ Ⓒ Ⓓ Ⓔ	12	Ⓐ Ⓑ Ⓒ Ⓓ Ⓔ	22	Ⓐ Ⓑ Ⓒ Ⓓ Ⓔ
3	Ⓐ Ⓑ Ⓒ Ⓓ Ⓔ	13	Ⓐ Ⓑ Ⓒ Ⓓ Ⓔ	23	Ⓐ Ⓑ Ⓒ Ⓓ Ⓔ
4	Ⓐ Ⓑ Ⓒ Ⓓ Ⓔ	14	Ⓐ Ⓑ Ⓒ Ⓓ Ⓔ	24	Ⓐ Ⓑ Ⓒ Ⓓ Ⓔ
5	Ⓐ Ⓑ Ⓒ Ⓓ Ⓔ	15	Ⓐ Ⓑ Ⓒ Ⓓ Ⓔ	25	Ⓐ Ⓑ Ⓒ Ⓓ Ⓔ
6	Ⓐ Ⓑ Ⓒ Ⓓ Ⓔ	16	Ⓐ Ⓑ Ⓒ Ⓓ Ⓔ	26	Ⓐ Ⓑ Ⓒ Ⓓ Ⓔ
7	Ⓐ Ⓑ Ⓒ Ⓓ Ⓔ	17	Ⓐ Ⓑ Ⓒ Ⓓ Ⓔ	27	Ⓐ Ⓑ Ⓒ Ⓓ Ⓔ
8	Ⓐ Ⓑ Ⓒ Ⓓ Ⓔ	18	Ⓐ Ⓑ Ⓒ Ⓓ Ⓔ	28	Ⓐ Ⓑ Ⓒ Ⓓ Ⓔ
9	Ⓐ Ⓑ Ⓒ Ⓓ Ⓔ	19	Ⓐ Ⓑ Ⓒ Ⓓ Ⓔ	29	Ⓐ Ⓑ Ⓒ Ⓓ Ⓔ
10	Ⓐ Ⓑ Ⓒ Ⓓ Ⓔ	20	Ⓐ Ⓑ Ⓒ Ⓓ Ⓔ	30	Ⓐ Ⓑ Ⓒ Ⓓ Ⓔ

SSAT Lower Level Practice Test 2

#	A B C D E	#	A B C D E	#	A B C D E
1	Ⓐ Ⓑ Ⓒ Ⓓ Ⓔ	11	Ⓐ Ⓑ Ⓒ Ⓓ Ⓔ	21	Ⓐ Ⓑ Ⓒ Ⓓ Ⓔ
2	Ⓐ Ⓑ Ⓒ Ⓓ Ⓔ	12	Ⓐ Ⓑ Ⓒ Ⓓ Ⓔ	22	Ⓐ Ⓑ Ⓒ Ⓓ Ⓔ
3	Ⓐ Ⓑ Ⓒ Ⓓ Ⓔ	13	Ⓐ Ⓑ Ⓒ Ⓓ Ⓔ	23	Ⓐ Ⓑ Ⓒ Ⓓ Ⓔ
4	Ⓐ Ⓑ Ⓒ Ⓓ Ⓔ	14	Ⓐ Ⓑ Ⓒ Ⓓ Ⓔ	24	Ⓐ Ⓑ Ⓒ Ⓓ Ⓔ
5	Ⓐ Ⓑ Ⓒ Ⓓ Ⓔ	15	Ⓐ Ⓑ Ⓒ Ⓓ Ⓔ	25	Ⓐ Ⓑ Ⓒ Ⓓ Ⓔ
6	Ⓐ Ⓑ Ⓒ Ⓓ Ⓔ	16	Ⓐ Ⓑ Ⓒ Ⓓ Ⓔ	26	Ⓐ Ⓑ Ⓒ Ⓓ Ⓔ
7	Ⓐ Ⓑ Ⓒ Ⓓ Ⓔ	17	Ⓐ Ⓑ Ⓒ Ⓓ Ⓔ	27	Ⓐ Ⓑ Ⓒ Ⓓ Ⓔ
8	Ⓐ Ⓑ Ⓒ Ⓓ Ⓔ	18	Ⓐ Ⓑ Ⓒ Ⓓ Ⓔ	28	Ⓐ Ⓑ Ⓒ Ⓓ Ⓔ
9	Ⓐ Ⓑ Ⓒ Ⓓ Ⓔ	19	Ⓐ Ⓑ Ⓒ Ⓓ Ⓔ	29	Ⓐ Ⓑ Ⓒ Ⓓ Ⓔ
10	Ⓐ Ⓑ Ⓒ Ⓓ Ⓔ	20	Ⓐ Ⓑ Ⓒ Ⓓ Ⓔ	30	Ⓐ Ⓑ Ⓒ Ⓓ Ⓔ

SSAT Lower Level

Quantitative Practice Test 1

30 questions

Total time for this test: 30 Minutes

You may NOT use a calculator for this test.

1. In the following figure, the shaded squares are what fractional part of the whole set of squares?

    A) $\frac{1}{2}$

    B) $\frac{5}{8}$

    C) $\frac{2}{3}$

    D) $\frac{3}{5}$

    E) $\frac{6}{11}$

2. Which of the following is greater than $\frac{12}{8}$?

    A) $\frac{1}{2}$

    B) $\frac{5}{2}$

    C) $\frac{3}{4}$

    D) 1

    E) 1.4

3. If $\frac{1}{3}$ of a number is greater than 8, the number must be .....

    A) Less than 4
    B) Equal to 16
    C) Equal to 24
    D) Greater than 24
    E) Equal to 32

4. If $4 \times (M + N) = 20$ and M is greater than 0, then N could Not be .....
   A) 1
   B) 2
   C) 3
   D) 4
   E) 5

5. Which of the following is closest to 5.03?
   A) 6
   B) 5.5
   C) 5
   D) 5.4
   E) 6.5

6. At a Zoo, the ratio of lions to tigers is 10 to 6. Which of the following could NOT be the total number of lions and tigers in the zoo?
   A) 64
   B) 80
   C) 98
   D) 104
   E) 160

7. In the multiplication bellow, A represents which digit?
   $$14 \times 3A2 = 4,788$$
   A) 2
   B) 3
   C) 4
   D) 6
   E) 8

8. If N is an even number, which of the following is always an odd number?
   A) $\frac{N}{2}$
   B) $N + 4$
   C) $2N$
   D) $(2 \times N) + 2$
   E) $N + 1$

9. $8.9 - 4.08$ is closest to which of the following.
   A) 4.1
   B) 4.8
   C) 6
   D) 8
   E) 13

$$x = 2,456 \qquad y = 259$$

10. Numbers x and y are shown above. How many times larger is the value of digit 5 in the number x, than the value of digit 5 in the number y?
    A) 1
    B) 10
    C) 100
    D) 1,000
    E) 10,000

11. If 5 added to a number, the sum is 20. If the same number added to 25, the answer is
    A) 30
    B) 35
    C) 40
    D) 45
    E) 50

12. $\frac{2+5+6\times1+1}{3+5} = ?$
    A) $\frac{15}{8}$
    B) $\frac{4}{8}$
    C) $\frac{7}{4}$
    D) $\frac{6}{8}$
    E) $\frac{10}{8}$

13. What is the Area of the square shown in the following square?
    A) 2
    B) 4
    C) 6
    D) 8
    E) 10

14. If 20 can be divided by both 4 and x without leaving a remainder, then 20 can also be divided by which of the following?
    A) $x + 4$
    B) $2x - 4$
    C) $x - 2$
    D) $x \times 4$
    E) $x + 1$

15. Use the equations below to answer the question:
$$x - 12 = 18$$
$$16 + y = 21$$

    What is the value of $x + y$?

    A) 9
    B) 10
    C) 11
    D) 12
    E) 14

16. Which of the following expressions has the same value as $\frac{5}{4} \times \frac{6}{2}$?
    A) $\frac{6 \times 3}{4}$
    B) $\frac{6 \times 2}{4}$
    C) $\frac{5 \times 6}{4}$
    D) $\frac{5 \times 3}{4}$
    E) $\frac{8 \times 3}{4}$

17. When 5 is added to three times number N, the result is 41. Then N is ….
    A) 11
    B) 12
    C) 14
    D) 16
    E) 18

18. At noon, the temperature was 15 degrees. By midnight, it had dropped another 20 degrees. What was the temperature at midnight?
    A) 10 degrees above zero
    B) 10 degrees below zero
    C) 5 degrees above zero
    D) 5 degrees below zero
    E) 15 degrees below zero

19. If a triangle has a base of 5 cm and a height of 8 cm, what is the area of the triangle?
    A) $15 cm^2$
    B) $20 cm^2$
    C) $40 cm^2$
    D) $45 cm^2$
    E) $50 cm^2$

20. Which formula would you use to find the area of a square?
    A) $length \times width \times height$
    B) $\frac{1}{2} base \times height$
    C) $length \times width$
    D) $side \times side$
    E) $\frac{1}{2}(length \times width \times heigt)$

21. What is the next number in this sequence?   2, 5, 9, 14, 20, ...
    A) 27
    B) 26
    C) 25
    D) 21
    E) 20

22. What is the average of the following numbers?   6, 10, 12, 23, 45
    A) 19
    B) 19.2
    C) 19.5
    D) 20
    E) 25

23. If there are 8 red balls and 12 blue balls in a basket, what is the probability that John will pick out a red ball from the basket?
    A) $\frac{18}{10}$
    B) $\frac{2}{5}$
    C) $\frac{2}{10}$
    D) $\frac{3}{5}$
    E) $\frac{20}{10}$

24. How many lines of symmetry does an equilateral triangle have?
    A) 5
    B) 4
    C) 3
    D) 2
    E) 1

25. What is %10 of 200?
    A) 10
    B) 20
    C) 30
    D) 40
    E) 50

26. Which of the following statement is False?
    A) $2 \times 2 = 4$
    B) $(4 + 1) \times 5 = 25$
    C) $6 \div (3 - 1) = 1$
    D) $6 \times (4 - 2) = 12$
    E) $(10 + 23) \times 10 = 330$

27. If all the sides in the following figure are of equal length and length of one side is 4, what is the perimeter of the figure?
    A) 15
    B) 18
    C) 20
    D) 24
    E) 28

28. $\frac{4}{5} - \frac{3}{5} = ?$
    A) 0.3
    B) 0.35
    C) 0.2
    D) 0.25
    E) 0.1

29. If $N = 2$ and $\frac{64}{N} + 4 = \square$, then $\square$ = ...
   A) 30
   B) 32
   C) 34
   D) 36
   E) 38

30. Four people can paint 4 houses in 10 days. How many people are needed to paint 8 houses in 5 days?
   A) 6
   B) 8
   C) 12
   D) 16
   E) 20

SSAT Lower Level

Quantitative Practice Test 2

30 questions

Total time for this test: 30 Minutes

You may NOT use a calculator for this test.

1. $\frac{8}{2} - \frac{3}{2} = ?$

   A) 1
   B) 1.5
   C) 2
   D) 2.5
   E) 3

2. If $48 = 3 \times N + 12$, then $N = \ldots$
   A) 8
   B) 12
   C) 14
   D) 15
   E) 20

3. The area of each square in the following shape is $8cm^2$. What is the area of shaded squares?
   A) $40cm^2$
   B) $42cm^2$
   C) $44cm^2$
   D) $45cm^2$
   E) $46cm^2$

4. What is the value of x in the following math equation?
   $$\frac{x}{15} + 9 = 11$$

   A) 15
   B) 20
   C) 25
   D) 35
   E) 30

5. When 3 is added to four times a number N, the result is 23. Which of the following equations represents this statement?
   A) $4 + 3N = 23$
   B) $23N + 4 = 3$
   C) $4N + 3 = 23$
   D) $4N + 23 = 3$
   E) $3N + 23 = 4$

6. When 78 is divided by 5, the remainder is the same as when 45 is divided by
   A) 2
   B) 4
   C) 5
   D) 7
   E) 9

7. John has 2,400 cards and Max has 606 cards. How many more cards does John have than Max?
   A) 1,794
   B) 1,798
   C) 1,812
   D) 1,828
   E) 1,994

8. In the following right triangle, what is the value of x?
   A) 15
   B) 30
   C) 45
   D) 60
   E) It cannot be determined from the information given

9. What is 5 percent of 480?
   A) 20
   B) 24
   C) 30
   D) 40
   E) 44

10. In a basket, the ratio of red marbles to blue marbles is 3 to 2. Which of the following could NOT be the total number of red and blue marbles in the basket?
    A) 15
    B) 32
    C) 55
    D) 60
    E) 70

11. A square has an area of $81 cm^2$. What is its perimeter?
    A) $28\ cm^2$
    B) $32\ cm^2$
    C) $34\ cm^2$
    D) $36\ cm^2$
    E) $54\ cm^2$

12. Find the missing number in the sequence: 5, 8, 12, ..., 23
    A) 15
    B) 17
    C) 18
    D) 20
    E) 22

13. The length of a rectangle is 3 times of its width. If the length is 18, what is the perimeter of the rectangle?
    A) 24
    B) 30
    C) 36
    D) 48
    E) 56

14. Mary has y dollars. John has $10 more than Mary. If John gives Mary $12, then in terms of y, how much does John have now?
    A) $y + 1$
    B) $y + 10$
    C) $y - 2$
    D) $y - 1$
    E) $y + 3$

15. Dividing 107 by 6 leaves a remainder of
    A) 1
    B) 2
    C) 3
    D) 4
    E) 5

16. If $6,000 + A - 200 = 7,400$, then $A =$
    A) 200
    B) 600
    C) 1,600
    D) 2,200
    E) 3,000

17. For what price is 15 percent off the same as $75 off?
    A) $200
    B) $300
    C) $350
    D) $400
    E) $500

18. Which of the following fractions is less than $\frac{3}{2}$?
    A) 1.4
    B) $\frac{5}{2}$
    C) 3
    D) 2.8
    E) 3.2

19. Use the equation below to answer the question.
$$x + 3 = 6$$
$$2y = 8$$
    What is the value of $y - x$?

    A) 1
    B) 2
    C) 3
    D) 4
    E) 5

20. If $310 - x + 116 = 225$, then $x =$
    A) 101
    B) 156
    C) 201
    D) 211
    E) 310

21. Of the following, 25 percent of $43.99 is closest to
    A) $9.90
    B) $10.00
    C) $11.00
    D) $11.50
    E) $12.00

22. Solve.
    8.08 − 5.6 = ...
    A) 2.42
    B) 2.46
    C) 2.48
    D) 3
    E) 3.2

23. If 500 + □ − 180 = 1,100, then □ = ?
    A) 580
    B) 660
    C) 700
    D) 780
    E) 900

24. There are 60 students in a class. If the ratio of the number of girls to the total number of students in the class is $\frac{1}{6}$, which are the following is the number of boys in that class?
    A) 10
    B) 20
    C) 25
    D) 40
    E) 50

25. If $N \times (5 − 3) = 12$ then $N =$?
    A) 6
    B) 12
    C) 13
    D) 14
    E) 18

26. If $x \blacksquare y = 3x + y - 2$, what is the value of $4 \blacksquare 12$?
   A) 4
   B) 18
   C) 22
   D) 36
   E) 48

27. Of the following, which number if the greatest?
   A) 0.092
   B) 0.8913
   C) 0.8923
   D) 0.8896
   E) 0.88

28. $\frac{7}{8} - \frac{3}{4} =$
   A) 0.125
   B) 0.375
   C) 0.5
   D) 0.625
   E) 0.775

29. Which of the following is the closest to 4.02?
   A) 4
   B) 4.2
   C) 4.3
   D) 4.5
   E) 3.5

30. Which of the following statements is False?
    A) $(7 \times 2 + 14) \times 2 = 56$
    B) $(2 \times 5 + 4) \div 2 = 7$
    C) $3 + (3 \times 6) = 21$
    D) $4 \times (3 + 9) = 48$
    E) $14 \div (2 + 5) = 5$

SSAT LOWER LEVEL Math
Practice Tests
Answers and Explanations

SSAT Lower Level Quantitative Practice Tests Answer Key

Quantitative Practice Test 1					Quantitative Practice Test 2			
1	D	16	D	1	D	16	C
2	B	17	B	2	B	17	E
3	D	18	D	3	A	18	A
4	E	19	B	4	E	19	A
5	C	20	D	5	C	20	C
6	C	21	A	6	D	21	C
7	C	22	B	7	A	22	C
8	E	23	B	8	C	23	D
9	B	24	C	9	B	24	E
10	A	25	B	10	B	25	A
11	C	26	C	11	D	26	C
12	C	27	D	12	B	27	C
13	B	28	C	13	D	28	A
14	D	29	D	14	C	29	A
15	C	30	D	15	E	30	E

Score Your Test

SSAT scores are broken down by its three sections: Verbal, Quantitative (or Math), and Reading. A sum of the three sections is also reported.

For the SSAT lower level, the score range is 300-600, the lowest possible score a student can earn is 300 and the highest score is 600 for each section. A student receives 1 point for every correct answer. For SSAT Lower Level, there is no penalty for wrong answers. That means that you can calculate the raw score by adding together the number of right answers.

The total scaled score for a Lower Level SSAT is the sum of the scores for the quantitative, verbal, and reading sections. A student will also receive a percentile score of between 1-99% that compares that student's test scores with those of other test takers of same grade and gender from the past 3 years.

Use the following table to convert SSAT Lower Level Quantitative Reasoning raw score to scaled score.

SSAT Lowe Level Quantitative Reasoning raw score to scaled score

Raw Scores	Scaled Scores
Below 10	Below 400
11 − 15	410 − 450
16 − 20	560 − 500
21 − 25	510 − 550
26 − 30	560 − 600

SSAT Lower Level Quantitative Practice Tests Explanations

SSAT Lower Level Quantitative Practice Test 1

1. **Choice D is correct.**

   There are 10 squares and 6 of them are shaded. Therefore, 6 out of 10 or $\frac{6}{10} = \frac{3}{5}$ are shaded.

2. **Choice B is correct.**

   $\frac{12}{8} = 1.5$, the only option that is greater than 1.5 is $\frac{5}{2}$.
   $$\frac{5}{2} = 2.5 , 2.5 > 1.5$$

3. **Choice D is correct.**

   If $\frac{1}{3}$ of a number is greater than 8, the number must be greater than 24.
   $$\frac{1}{3}x > 8 \rightarrow \text{multiply both sides of the inequality by 3, then: } x > 24$$

4. **Choice E is correct.**

   $4 \times (M + N) = 20$, then $M + N = 5$. $M > 0 \rightarrow N$ could not be 5

5. **Choice C is correct.**

   The closest to 5.03 is 5 in the options provided.

6. **Choice C is correct.**

   The ratio of lions to tigers is 10 to 6 or 5 to 3 at the zoo. Therefore, total number of lions and tigers must be divisible by 8.
   $$5 + 3 = 8$$
   From the numbers provided, only 98 is not divisible by 8.

7. **Choice C is correct.**

   A represents digit 4 in the multiplication.
   $$14 \times 342 = 4{,}788$$

8. **Choice E is correct.**

   N is even. Let's choose 2 and 4 for N. Now, let's review the options provided.

   A) $\frac{N}{2} = \frac{2}{2} = 1, \quad \frac{N}{2} = \frac{4}{2} = 2,$ One result is odd and the other one is even.
   B) $N + 4 = 2 + 4 = 6, 4 + 4 = 8$ Both results are even.
   C) $2N = 2 \times 2 = 4, 4 \times 2 = 8$ Both results are even.
   D) $(2 \times N) + 2 = (2 \times 2) + 2 = 6, (4 \times 2) + 2 = 10$ Both results are even.
   E) $N + 1 = 2 + 1 = 3, 4 + 1 = 5$ Both results are odd.

9. **Choice B is correct.**

   $8.9 - 4.08 = 4.82$, which is closest to 4.8

10. **Choice A is correct.**

    The value of digit 5 in both numbers x and y are in the tens place. Therefore, they have the same value.

11. **Choice C is correct.**

    $$5 + x = 20 \rightarrow x = 15 \rightarrow 15 + 25 = 40$$

12. **Choice C is correct.**

    $$\frac{2 + 5 + 6 \times 1 + 1}{5 + 3} = \frac{14}{8} = \frac{7}{4}$$

13. **Choice B is correct.**

    Area of a square = (one side) × (one side)
    $$2 \times 2 = 4$$

14. **Choice D is correct.**
$$20 = x \times 4 \to x = 20 \div 4 = 5$$
x equals to 5. Let's review the options provided:
A) $x + 4 \to 5 + 4 = 9$ 20 is not divisible by 9.
B) $2x - 4 \to 2 \times 5 - 4 = 6$ 20 is not divisible by 6.
C) $x - 2 \to 5 - 2 = 3$ 20 is not divisible by 3.
D) $x \times 4 \to 5 \times 4 = 20$ 20 is divisible by 20.
E) $x + 1 \to 5 + 1 = 6$ 20 is not divisible by 6.

The answer is D.

15. **Choice C is correct.**
$$x - 12 = 18 \to x = 6$$
$$16 + y = 21 \to y = 5$$
$$x + y = 6 + 5 = 11$$

16. **Choice D is correct.**
$$\frac{5}{4} \times \frac{6}{2} = \frac{30}{8} = \frac{15}{4}$$
Choice D is equal to $\frac{15}{4}$.
$$\frac{5 \times 3}{4} = \frac{15}{4}$$

17. **Choice B is correct.**
$$5 + 3N = 41 \to 3N = 41 - 5 = 36 \to N = 12$$

18. **Choice D is correct.**
$$15 - 20 = -5$$
The temperature at midnight was 5 degrees below zero.

19. **Choice B is correct.**
Area of a triangle $= \frac{1}{2} \times (base) \times (height) = \frac{1}{2} \times 5 \times 8 = 20$

20. **Choice D is correct.**
$$area\ of\ a\ square = side \times side$$

21. Choice A is correct.
$$2 + 3 = 5 \to 5 + 4 = 9 \to 9 + 5 = 14 \to 14 + 6 = 20 \to 20 + 7 = 27$$

22. Choice B is correct.
$$average = \frac{sum\ of\ all\ numbers}{number\ of\ numbers} = \frac{6 + 10 + 12 + 23 + 45}{5} = 19.2$$

23. Choice B is correct.
There are 8 red ball and 20 are total number of balls. Therefore, probability that John will pick out a red ball from the basket is 8 out of 20 or $\frac{8}{8+12} = \frac{8}{20} = \frac{2}{5}$.

24. Choice C is correct.
An equilateral triangle has 3 lines of symmetry.

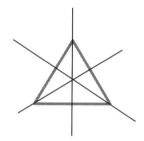

25. Choice B is correct.

10 percent of 200 = 10% of 200 = $\frac{10}{100} \times 200 = 20$

26. Choice C is correct.

Let's review the options provided:

A) $2 \times 2 = 4$ This is true!
B) $(4 + 1) \times 5 = 25$ This is true!
C) $6 \div (3 - 1) = 1 \to 6 \div 2 = 3$ This is NOT true!
D) $6 \times (4 - 2) = 12 \to 6 \times 2 = 12$ This is true!
E) $(10 + 23) \times 10 = 330 \to 33 \times 10 = 330$ This is true!

27. Choice D is correct.
The shape has 6 equal sides. And is side is 4. Then, the perimeter of the shape is:
$4 \times 6 = 24$

28. Choice C is correct.

$$\frac{4}{5} - \frac{3}{5} = \frac{1}{5} = 0.2$$

29. Choice D is correct.

$N = 2$, then: $\frac{64}{2} + 4 = 32 + 4 = 36$

30. Choice D is correct.

Four people can paint 4 houses in 10 days. It means that for painting 8 houses in 10 days we need 8 people. To paint 8 houses in 5 days, 16 people are needed.

SSAT Lower Level Quantitative Practice Tests Explanations

SSAT Lower Level Quantitative Practice Test 2

1. **Choice D is correct.**
$$\frac{8}{2} - \frac{3}{2} = \frac{5}{2} = 2.5$$

2. **Choice B is correct.**
$$48 = 3 \times N + 12 \to 3N = 48 - 12 = 36 \to N = 12$$

3. **Choice A is correct.**

    There are 5 shaded squares. Then: $5 \times 8cm^2 = 40cm^2$

4. **Choice E is correct.**
$$\frac{x}{15} + 9 = 11 \to \frac{x}{15} = 11 - 9 = 2 \to \frac{x}{15} = 2 \to x = 15 \times 2 = 30$$

5. **Choice C is correct.**
$$3 + (4 \times N) = 23 \to 4N + 3 = 23$$

6. **Choice D is correct.**

    78 divided by 5, the remainder is 3. 45 divided by 7, the remainder is also 3.

7. **Choice A is correct.**
$$2,400 - 606 = 1,794$$

8. **Choice C is correct.**

   All angles in a triangle sum up to 180 degrees. The triangle provided is an isosceles triangle. In an isosceles triangle, the three angles are 45, 45, and 90 degrees. Therefore, the value of x is 45.

9. **Choice B is correct.**
$$5 \text{ percent of } 480 = \frac{5}{100} \times 480 = \frac{1}{20} \times 480 = \frac{480}{20} = 24$$

10. **Choice B is correct.**

    The ratio of red marbles to blue marbles is 3 to 2. Therefore, the total number of marbles must be divisible by 5.
    3 + 2 = 5
    32 is the only one that is not divisible by 5.

11. **Choice D is correct.**
$$Area\ of\ a\ square\ =\ side \times side = 81 \rightarrow side = 9$$
$$Perimeter\ of\ a\ square\ =\ 4 \times side\ =\ 4 \times 9 = 36$$

12. **Choice B is correct.**
$$5 + 3 = 8, \quad 8 + 4 = 12, \quad 12 + 5 = 17, \quad 17 + 6 = 23$$

13. **Choice D is correct.**

    The length of the rectangle is 18. Then, its width is 6.
    $$18 \div 3 = 6$$
    $$Perimeter\ of\ a\ rectangle = 2 \times width + 2 \times length = 2 \times 6 + 2 \times 18 = 12 + 36 = 48$$

14. **Choice C is correct.**
$$Mary's\ Money = y$$
$$John's\ Money = y + 10$$
$$John\ gives\ Mary\ \$12 \rightarrow y + 10 - 12 = y - 2$$

15. Choice E is correct.

Dividing 107 by 6 leaves a remainder of 5.

16. Choice C is correct.

$6,000 + A - 200 = 7,400 \rightarrow 6,000 + A = 7,400 + 200 = 7,600 \rightarrow A = 7,600 - 6,000 = 1,600$

17. Choice E is correct.

$75 off is the same as 15 percent off. Thus, 15 percent of a number is 75.

Then: $15\% \text{ of } x = 75 \rightarrow 0.15x = 75 \rightarrow x = \frac{75}{0.15} = 500$

18. Choice A is correct.

$$\frac{3}{2} = 1.5 > 1.4$$

19. Choice A is correct.

$$x + 3 = 6 \rightarrow x = 3$$
$$2y = 8 \rightarrow y = 4$$
$$y - x = 4 - 3 = 1$$

20. Choice C is correct.

$310 - x + 116 = 225 \rightarrow 310 - x = 225 - 116 = 109 \rightarrow x = 310 - 109 = 201$

21. Choice C is correct.

25 percent of $44.00 is $11. (Remember that 25 percent is equal to one fourth)

22. Choice C is correct.

$$8.08 - 5.6 = 2.48$$

23. Choice D is correct.

$$500 + \square - 180 = 1,100 \rightarrow 500 + \square = 1,100 + 180 = 1,280$$

$$\square = 1,280 - 500 = 780$$

24. Choice E is correct.

$\frac{1}{6}$ of students are girls. Therefore, $\frac{5}{6}$ of students in the class are boys. $\frac{5}{6}$ of 60 is 50. There are 50 boys in the class.

$$\frac{5}{6} \times 60 = \frac{300}{6} = 50$$

25. Choice A is correct.

$$N \times (5 - 3) = 12 \rightarrow N \times 2 = 12 \rightarrow N = 6$$

26. Choice C is correct.

If $x \blacksquare y = 3x + y - 2$, Then:
$$4 \blacksquare 12 = 3(4) + 12 - 2 = 12 + 12 - 2 = 22$$

27. Choice C is correct.

Of the numbers provided, 0.8923 is the greatest.

28. Choice A is correct.

$$\frac{7}{8} - \frac{3}{4} = \frac{7}{8} - \frac{6}{8} = \frac{1}{8} = 0.125$$

29. Choice A is correct.

The closest number to 4.02 is 4.

30. Choice E is correct.

$14 \div (2 + 5) = 14 \div 7 = 2$ not 5

"Effortless Math" Publications

Effortless Math authors' team strives to prepare and publish the best quality Mathematics learning resources to make learning Math easier for all. We hope that our publications help you or your student Math in an effective way.

We all in Effortless Math wish you good luck and successful studies!

Effortless Math Authors

www.EffortlessMath.com

... So Much More Online!

- ✓ FREE Math lessons

- ✓ More Math learning books!

- ✓ Mathematics Worksheets

- ✓ Online Math Tutors

Need a PDF version of this book?

Please visit www.EffortlessMath.com

Made in the USA
Middletown, DE
25 August 2019